AN EXTRAORDINARILY ORDINARY LIFE

LESSONS
LEARNED

An
Extraordinarily
Ordinary Life

TIM CARLIN

LIONCREST
PUBLISHING

AN EXTRAORDINARILY ORDINARY LIFE
Lessons Learned

ISBN   978-1-5445-0959-4 *Hardcover*
   978-1-5445-0958-7 *Paperback*
   978-1-5445-0957-0 *Ebook*

This book is dedicated to my clients.

"You will never truly know yourself or the strength of your relationships until both have been tested by adversity." —J. K. Rowling

Contents

Introduction

When I was a sophomore at Canisius High School in Buffalo, New York, my teacher, Vincent Chiumento, had our class read a book that changed my life: *The Once and Future King* by T. H. White. It told the tale of King Arthur and the Knights of the Round Table, and it quickly became one of my favorites. Every so often, I read it again, and I always get something new out of the experience.

My favorite part is when Merlin turns a young boy, Arthur (then known as Wart), into a fish, then a bird, and then an ant, teaching Arthur lessons to prepare him to be a good and righteous king. Arthur learns the essential lesson that might is for doing right, not that might makes right.

What resonates most heavily with me is how the author depicts Arthur's rise, his fall, and then his rise again. We all have rises and falls in our own stories; I know it's been a common theme throughout my life.

After studying at Canisius, I went to West Point, then into the Army, and then to Ranger School—the rise of the military man. After eight years of doing might for right, I left the Army and joined the Pepsi-Cola Company in Kansas City while serving in the Kansas National Guard on weekends.

Me with the Pepsi "Uh-Huh" Girls.

That gave rise to my time as a franchise operations director for PepsiCo, the corporate owner of Taco Bell, Pizza Hut, and KFC at the time, before getting recruited as a national director for Philips 66. I rose ever higher—becoming a national restaurant consultant in Chicago—before falling from great heights, getting laid off during the 2001 recession.

After that, my life rose in a new direction: I learned to dance, met the woman who would become my wife, and traveled the world before deciding to move back to Overland Park, Kansas, and starting over as a financial advisor for Edward Jones. In the first two-and-a-half years, I went from zero dollars to $40 million by going door to door and asking people to do business with me. Since then, I've built my business to $200 million while giving away $80 million to help six new advisors start their businesses while being mentored for a year or two in my office. During my Jones tenure, I created fourteen well-paying jobs in my city as I built a team that was one of the top five offices based on production and client satisfaction as ranked by JD Power.

In November 2019, I became a registered independent advisor and partner with V Wealth Advisors in Overland Park, Kansas. As a certified financial planner with fiduciary responsibility to my clients, it was a natural step in my growth and reinvention to better serve others.

Like King Arthur, I've had my share of battles and troubles in life. Ultimately, my goal is still to do good and to strive and help as many people as I can.

WOULD YOU LIKE FRIES WITH THAT?

People often ask, "How did you get from the military into the restaurant business and then into financial planning?"

My military experience taught me to access a tremendous amount of information and to use it to make good decisions, primarily so I wouldn't get people killed. Going from that level of responsibility to making sure that customers didn't get fried chicken when they ordered tacos was an entirely different order of business, yet the same skills applied. Whether leading troops or getting slammed with a rush at Taco Bell, you have to be prepared. What staff do you need? Where do they need to be positioned? What happens if you have more people coming through the drive-through than you expected?

The lessons of leadership I learned in the military have served me throughout my life, most recently in my role as a certified financial planner. I'm able to be proactive, look at the facts and assumptions of a situation, and say, "The market is going to do one of three things: go up, go down, or trade sideways." Based on my client's family's situation, I can prepare a course of action for each possibility.

My experience keeping troops from getting blown up helps me make sure my clients' accounts don't blow up when they're a year away from retirement. I apply everything I've learned along the way from my variety of experiences to the task at hand. It involves knowing the facts on the ground and thinking on your feet.

People who've done the same thing for fifty years are probably very good at what they do. Someone who has always been a kindergarten teacher only has that one perspective. A military officer who then becomes a contractor for the military has never known anything other than working for the government under very strict rules and regulations; they've always been told what to do. If you've always been in corporate America but you've never been an entrepreneur working on your own (or the reverse—an entrepreneur who has never worked for a larger corporation or been in the military), you have developed a narrow focus through that one set of experiences.

Problems can arise, though, when the world we know shifts and that person doesn't know how to relate what they know to other situations and to see the big picture. People who have done the same thing for many decades may have tremendous depth but not enough breadth of experience.

As a certified financial planner, it's important to have both breadth and depth—a wide number of experiences and deep knowledge in a particular area of expertise.

KEEP IT SIMPLE, STUPID

My goal in writing this book is to share my stories with you, whether you're a client, a friend, or a family member. I'm in the business of giving financial advice, providing counsel, and assisting people in decision-making. On these pages I hope to show you not only how I got here, but also what we all need to do in order to make rational decisions that bring us more enjoyment and benefits in life.

For example, I met with a couple recently who felt that their house was weighing them down. Trying to keep up with all the costs and effort of making their home picture-perfect kept them from seeing friends and having a good time. They were considering selling, but the value of houses in their area had gone down, and they didn't want to take a loss.

We talked about their overall situation and determined that, financially, they'd be fine selling their house. But we kept on talking until I discovered what was most important to them: having their family and loved ones around. Instead of focusing on what really mattered in their lives, they'd become overly absorbed in societal expectations, believing that their house had to be perfect. They just didn't know how to proceed.

As we talked, I helped them see that it's okay if their

house isn't perfect. More important to them was that the house simply be a comfortable place to entertain friends and family, to have fun and enjoy themselves, instead of worrying about making it a showpiece with perfectly arranged landscaping. Their core values were more about having a community of loved ones to share their home with. It was a simple solution that supported their social nature, instead of striving to keep up with a lifestyle that wasn't really theirs.

After that, they looked at their house from a different perspective. Rather than seeing it as a burden that prevented them from being able to enjoy time with others, their home became a place for people to come together.

Many of us make life more complicated than it has to be. Instead of striving for perfection, I've found it's far better to strive for what's good. As you'll soon see, I've never been close to perfect in my life.

AN ORDINARY GUY

I grew up in Buffalo, New York, which is an ordinary city. There is nothing sexy or extraordinary about Buffalo. It doesn't compare to Los Angeles, Chicago, or Miami. I came from a blue-collar family where there were no silver spoons. I learned to work for and appreciate everything I have.

My home when I was growing up.

I've had health issues, relationship issues, and business issues to battle through. Like many other people, I've been laid off and had to pick myself up and go on (unfortunately, getting laid off is an ordinary thing these days). What isn't ordinary, I suppose, is that after getting laid off, I went on to build a multimillion-dollar business by going door to door and talking to one prospect at a time. My background and experience led me to look setbacks in the eye, as I've had to look cancer in the eye, accept the challenge, and run marathons. I'm a chameleon—the Army Ranger who learned to ballroom dance and went on to become a gentleman host onboard the *Queen Elizabeth II.*

I believe that ordinary people like me can be far more than ordinary.

And you can too.

You may not identify with all the specifics of my stories, but I expect you'll see some of yourself in the stories I tell. I hope you'll find yourself reflected in these pages and that some of the lessons I've learned will ring true for you.

LESSONS LEARNED

This book is the (abridged) story of a life. As you read through, I hope you'll come to know me better as a person, gain insight through my experience, and apply some of what I've learned to the stories of your own life.

Here's a start on what's to come:

- **Be in service to others.** When you serve others, you put their needs before your own. And when you help others, especially those less fortunate than you, it makes you feel really good. It's a win-win.
- **Never stop learning.** We tend to just do what we're comfortable with. Walking a mile in others' shoes and experiencing things totally out of your world allows you to better understand other people's points of view, improves your communication with them, and teaches you how to serve them better.
- **Punch above your weight.** We all have strengths and weaknesses. We all experience challenges—and we can all strive to push even harder to meet those challenges. The trick is to neutralize our weaknesses and

turn them into strengths. You're going to experience problems you didn't expect and can't imagine right now. Don't give in to anger and frustration at that roadblock. Instead, find a constructive way to channel that energy into overcoming the setback. Working hard allows you to punch above your weight—the harder you work, the higher you can punch. You can turn it into a superpower for making a difference for yourself and others.

▸ **Never stand still.** Never standing still means always trying to improve and learn new things, being fearless and confident, and pushing the envelope. When you do things that make you uncomfortable, sometimes you fail and other times you succeed, but either way you learn something that allows you to grow and develop.

▸ **Think long term.** We all want to have our needs met, to feel secure and protected. When we're younger, we think about who we want to become when we grow up. Part of that is learning what to do in order to have what's important to us. We can prepare now for the long term by choosing to follow a course of action and to gain the knowledge and experience we need to get there.

▸ **Reinvent yourself.** If you don't continuously reinvent yourself, you become obsolete. When you do reinvent yourself, you change to stay relevant in the environment and situation around you, and you survive and thrive.

▸ **Don't follow the crowd.** Getting stuck in group-think closes your mind to different ideas. When you can think on your own, you're much more likely to make a better decision. Seeing the whole picture, all 360 degrees, requires keeping an open mind.

▸ **You have to give to receive.** One of the greatest things we can do is give back to others. It allows you to impact the world in your own small, special way, and every little bit adds up. Giving back makes our country and the world a better place to live.

MAKE THE ORDINARY EXTRAORDINARY

I hope that reading these stories and discovering how I learned these lessons and skills for decision-making will serve as inspiration along the way.

Before you continue with the rest of the book, I want to thank you for giving your time to reading my story. Time is one of our most precious resources, and I appreciate you using that resource to learn more about who I am, where I come from, and what I can offer.

I hope to show how the ordinary can, in fact, be extraordinary. I'm not anyone special, but it it's very special to me that you're reading this book.

If I can inspire you to get through a tough time, a difficult problem, or a decision in your life right now, then I'll know that writing this book was worth it. If some of my stories make you laugh or provide you with some perspective or hope, then I'll be satisfied. If what I share motivates you to devote yourself more to helping the people around you, then we'll all be the better for it.

I hope that I can be in service to you. And that's where my story starts—being in service to others.

CHAPTER 1

Be in Service
to Others

Raised Catholic, I grew up with an appreciation of God
and Jesus. I had faith that they were real, just like Santa
Claus was real to me as a child.

My family, circa 1985.

Although I don't still believe in Santa, my faith in God is just as important to me today as it was then. It comforts me to know that even though there are plenty of bad things going on in the world, there are still a lot of good things too.

When I received my First Communion, I learned that the altar was a very special place—I was told that Jesus actually became present on the altar. So when I got a chance to be an altar boy, in the sixth grade, I jumped at it. I knew it would be a great way to help the priest serve others through communion and by making sure that he had all the things he needed for Mass.

Many people attended the early service, at six in the morning, before their workday. My house was about a mile away, so I would wake up early, get dressed in the dark, and walk through the deserted streets to Assumption Church. In winter, when snow had fallen over Buffalo, my boots crunched on the ice. It was cold, but I stopped to admire the beautiful, crystal-white snow.

Under the command and control of Sister Lydia. (That's me with the bow tie!)

Then I walked up to the old, European-style, gothic, brick church. It was so vast and cavernous, I felt like the Hunchback of Notre Dame could be hiding somewhere in the shadows as I walked past the big organ.

The first few times I helped the priest, my heart was pounding in my chest. As the priest and I walked out in procession, I was sure people could see my heart beating through my robes. During the blessing of the body and blood of Christ, I wanted to make sure I was right on cue; I had to ring the chimes at *exactly* the right time when the priest raised the host or the chalice. I didn't want to hit the chimes early by accident or ring them again after they should be silent.

When we reached the front of the church, we bowed, and I took my place next to the priest as he spoke to the congregation. I stood when I was supposed to stand and sat when I was supposed to sit. I knelt during prayers. Then it was time. When the priest raised the host (sacramental bread) as a blessing on behalf of Jesus, I picked up the chimes that were on the floor next to my knee and shook them—but I had to set the chimes down right away, to stop the sound so they didn't ring too long or too short. The priest lowered the host and continued the Mass. Then he raised the wine, and I rang the chimes again—right on cue. The three little bells chimed out, and I could hear the sound ring throughout the church. After that, I was in good shape for the rest of the service. *Whew.*

When it was time for the priest to give the host to the congregation, I escorted him and held a little gold plate on a wooden handle under the chin of the person taking communion. At the time, it hadn't yet been approved for the priest to put the host in the person's hand; it had to be placed on the tongue. I knew my role was so important because if the person dropped the body of Christ, I didn't want it to fall on the ground; I would catch it on the plate. I felt proud to help administer the blood and body of Christ. I wasn't nervous anymore; instead, my chest puffed out with the importance of my sacred duty. That pious moment each person shared in communion with the Lord felt very meaningful and personal, so the interaction was a big deal for me.

During the Lenten season, I would walk the Stations of the Cross and listen to the priest tell the story of the rise, the fall, and then the rise of Jesus. That story always reminded me of the King Arthur tale I mentioned in the introduction—the rise, fall, and rise again of the future king.

Being an altar boy also meant going with the priest to do funeral duty at the two funeral homes near our church. The priest blessed the body and administered the sacrament for the dead. During these blessings, the caskets were open, and I wasn't afraid to look down at the bodies. The people looked real, almost alive—but at the same time not. The pallor of their skin, their stillness, and something indescribable but obvious vividly highlighted this difference to me.

I realized there was a big transformative event happening as people said their goodbyes. I saw that death was a part of life. I was too young to really understand mortality at the time, but I was so proud of helping the priest administer to the community, taking care of people's loved ones according to their faith, and being there for the folks at my church.

PUT OTHERS' NEEDS IN FRONT OF YOUR OWN

Being an altar boy set me up for future service, at West Point, in the Army, and serving my clients today.

As an altar boy, I learned of this higher power who gave his life so we can all be better. There's redemption there. Today, I seek out organizations to get involved with that help people, so I can continue to be a servant in those faith-based organizations.

I have always felt good serving others. It gives a sense of rhythm, duty, and honor to my life, and my early service gave me a solid foundational understanding of the cycle of life and what it means to help other people. I learned what was good and right.

As I told you, *The Once and Future King* was a huge influence in my life. I got picked on in sixth grade, but I got stronger by learning judo, wrestling, and working out. I didn't use that to pick on other people, though—I used it to help people.

The military was an extension of that concept. I wasn't joining the military to go bully other people but to be in service and to help others. My extended family were first responders, firemen and policemen, so that concept of public service and using might for right was built in by my family.

Being in service to others creates a better world for all of us. It could be something as simple as smiling at someone or giving them a sincere compliment to make them feel happy. You can reward people with time, love, understanding, and listening. All of these contribute to making someone else's life a little better.

If we can all touch other people's lives—even if just in your own orbit—we can be part of a community and make life better for people as a whole. We are all small specks of sand on a beach that is far and wide; in the big scheme of things, one individual doesn't make that big a difference. However, in the short amount of time we're here on earth, we can make a tremendous difference with friends and family and clients—even strangers we come into contact with—by helping them feel better, serving at Mass or in the military, delivering humanitarian aid or comfort in a time of need, and providing stability and security when they need it most.

Nowhere did I learn this more than serving in the military, which began with my acceptance to the United States Military Academy at West Point.

WEST POINT BOUND

I knew in high school that I wanted to go to West Point. I worked toward that goal during my entire time at Canisius High School, a prestigious all-boys Jesuit school in Buffalo.

Canisius High is housed in a stone, gothic building that reminded me of King Arthur's castle.

Canisius High School.

The school's motto is fittingly "service to others." The Jesuits are like the special forces of the Catholic Church—

they're the ones who went through Europe to teach people about Christianity, but also about arts and letters, math, and science. They're the educators of the Catholic Church. With their influence, we did service projects such as providing meals for foster families, teaching inner city kids how to read and write, and helping Vietnam veterans repair their homes.

I knew that I also wanted to go to a prestigious college that would allow me to continue to provide service to people in need. When I learned about the history of West Point, it fit right into my Knights of the Round Table values on both a small and large scale. Ulysses S. Grant led with dignity during General Lee's surrender at Appomattox. He allowed the Southern soldiers to ride in with dignity, and he saluted them, showing them a proper display of courtesy and respect—not humiliation—for a fellow American opponent. That was definitely an example of might for right. I also thought of Blackjack Pershing, a West Point man himself, leading the first big expeditionary force in World War I. But perhaps the best example was General Eisenhower serving as a modern-day King Arthur as he planned the invasion of Western Europe. Generals Bradley and Patton then became Sir Lancelot and the other knights as they executed the plan to bring the war to a close.

At the time I attended West Point, the two major superpowers were the United States and the Soviet Union—good versus evil. From my point of view, I wanted to serve on the side of good.

Applying to West Point was a thrill for me. It's a long application process, plus we all had to be nominated by our congressmen or senators. A congressman or senator can each have up to five people they recommend going to each of the service academies, ensuring equal representation from all over the United States. When West Point was founded in 1802, the founding fathers wanted every congressional and senatorial district to have people attending the military academies and serving the country.

My congressman was John LaFalce. I didn't know him personally, but I interviewed with his service selection board in a ritual that occurs throughout the country—even to this day—on the first or second Saturday in December.

I also had to get a waiver for my eyesight, which made it even tougher to get in. Generally speaking, they want recruits to have good 20/20 vision, but my vision was 20/200—I was legally blind. Dr. Gladys, my optometrist, gave me a little bit of leeway in taking my test. He didn't fudge the numbers, but he allowed me to pull my eyelid, which flattened my eyeballs, so my astigmatism didn't interfere when I read the letters on the eye chart.

When I found out I got into West Point, I was so darn excited. I thanked Dr. Gladys profusely, promised to visit, and bought him a West Point sweatshirt for his support.

I knew I was going to get hazed, but it was all so exciting that I didn't even care—I couldn't wait to begin my experience.

My report date was July 5, 1978. On Independence Day, my mom; dad; brother, Jeff; sister, Roxane; and I got into the station wagon and drove from Buffalo to Newburgh, New York, which is about forty-five minutes outside West Point. We stayed in a hotel the night before, swimming in the pool and going out for a nice dinner. I got little sleep that night because I knew that I was starting my West Point career the very next day.

WELCOME TO WEST POINT

When we arrived, we were directed to the football stadium. An officer addressed us briefly, giving us an introduction and overview of West Point, then said, "Please take one minute to say goodbye to your parents."

He started the clock.

After one minute—exactly—was up, he said, "New cadets, report to the buses down below the stadium."

We gathered our gear, and off we went to the buses. Before we got on, we were met by "the man in the red sash"—an upper-class cadet who was empowered to begin teaching us how to be West Pointers.

I stepped up to the bus, and the man in the red sash said, "Drop your bag."

I dropped my bag.

"Pick your bag up."

I picked it up.

"Drop your bag."

Again, I did as I was told.

"What's your name?"

"Tim."

"No, it's not."

"Tim Carlin?"

"From now on, your name is New Cadet Carlin. New Cadet Carlin, what are your four responses?"

"I—I don't know."

"The only four responses you can answer when being addressed by an upper-class cadet are, 'Yes, sir,' 'No, sir,' 'No excuse, sir,' and 'Sir, I do not know.'"

"Yes, sir," I replied hesitantly. Then, without thinking, I picked up my bag.

"Who told you to pick up your bag?" he demanded.

"No one, sir."

"Is that one of your four responses?"

"No, sir! No excuse, sir."

And on it went. I wasn't even a cadet—I was a new cadet until I graduated from Plebe Summer, also known as Beast Barracks.

The whole concept back then was to break us down and build us back up, simulating conditions we'd have to face and teaching us to function under pressure and stress.

We began to get conditioned on how to think, what to do, how to react. Ultimately, I realized that I was no longer a civilian; I was at West Point, the United States Military

Academy, the premier leadership institution for US Army officers in the world—and I belonged to them now.

We marched off and began the assembly line: getting vaccinated; picking up our uniforms, which consisted of black shorts with gold piping, a white t-shirt, and black socks with black oxfords; and having our hair cut—either a high-and-tight or all shaved off, which we called baldy sour. That's what I chose. Then they taught us how to march so that, by the end of the day, we could have a parade for the parents.

During this time, the parents were off taking a tour of the academy, getting briefed, and seeing museums. We were behind the scenes learning how to be soldiers the very first day. We reported at nine o'clock, and by five o'clock in the afternoon all 1,100 new cadets were in formation marching to music in front of parents in full uniform.

Later, my dad said, laughing, "When you guys were marching off to the mess hall, they slammed the door shut after the last cadet walked in. It was like pigs to slaughter."

Boy, was he right! When it was time for dinner, we sat ten people per table with the upperclassmen at the front of the table. I saw this delicious family-style meal in front of me with huge portions that we could serve ourselves.

But with all the yelling and screaming from the upper-classmen—"Sit one fist-width away from the back of your chair!" "Look at the academy crest at the twelve o'clock position of your plate!" "Do not look anywhere else unless you are addressed by an upperclassman!"—we didn't get to eat more than three bites the whole meal.

BECOMING A PLEBE

The mess hall looked exactly like Hogwarts in the *Harry Potter* movies. Before there was Hogwarts, there was West Point—and Canisius High School even looked like a small version, a miniature Hogwarts. Of course, I didn't know that then, but as soon as I saw Hogwarts in the first movie, I immediately thought, "That's West Point. I went to Hogwarts!"

The West Point mess hall displays pictures of old professors and generals from years gone by, including the Revolutionary and Civil Wars. There are different wings of the mess hall where the different companies sit. Each company has a different mascot and name. For example, my company was Company H-4, and our mascot was a charging hog. When we would greet each other within the company, we would say, "Go Hogs, sir!"

All around me, I could feel the history. I thought of the famous people who had gone through West Point, even people who weren't in the military, like Mark Twain and Edgar Allan Poe. West Point is like Harvard and the other old-school, Ivy League institutions. I felt that I had entered into an amazing historical experience.

West Point even uses a different nomenclature for students:

▶ All students are called cadets.
▶ First-year cadets are not called freshmen but plebes.
▶ Second-year cadets are known as yearlings.
▶ Third-year cadets are cows.
▶ Fourth-year cadets are firsties because they are first at the head of the line.

West Point first class photo.

I thought I was prepared because I had studied the system, but I kept thinking, "I can't wait until plebe year is over, but now it's just day one."

I was very scared, but also proud, because I knew I had what it took to get through this. It wasn't always easy, and there were times when I would break down, but I knew I was exactly where I wanted to be.

It did get better, but Plebe Summer is when they try to weed out the weak. Of the 1,100 people who started with me, only 750 graduated four years later.

As a plebe, I was assigned a room with Tom Davitt and Ray Iram, then with George Kunkle second semester. I became good buddies with them, just as I did with the other roommates I went on to have at West Point: Mark Kondry, Dave Ziglar, Phil Pierson, and Nencho Kolev, a kid of Bulgarian background also from Buffalo.

West Point is a military academy, so we learned about warfare and being soldiers, but we also took regular college classes—anywhere from nineteen to twenty-three credit hours a semester. As a plebe and yearling, we went to school Monday through Saturday. It was a grueling program, but we all ended up with a great education.

TRAINING TIME

During the end of Plebe Summer, we learned pugil stick fighting to simulate bayonet training.

The football team taught bayonet training because it was good duty for them—plus, they were the biggest guys on campus. At that point in time, I was 145 pounds and some of them were 280, so it was a significant weight difference between the person whacking me with a pugil stick and me, the one getting whacked.

As the final test of bayonet training, we had to complete a course—like a Tough Mudder endurance obstacle course, except that we had to get through big guys in helmets holding pugil sticks simulating bayonets on the end of a rifle. We had to run up hills while they simulated machine gun fire, artillery simulators, and smoke grenades, teaching us to charge the enemy in hand-to-hand combat. It was an experience like no other I had ever been through up to that point in my life.

We also had to show what we knew from bayonet training; like a sword fight, there were certain strokes we had to learn. They would call out a stroke, and we'd have to execute it. Then they'd give a counterstroke, and we'd have to execute that as well.

The word around our barracks was that you didn't want to get Bam-Bam, a nose-tackle on the football team, for the bayonet test. Bam-Bam was big, he was mean, he was tough—he was every new cadet's nightmare.

When it was my turn for the test, I ran in a lane about a quarter-mile long, up and down hills and tough terrain, full of smoke in the middle of the course. I was in a valley, choking and coughing and trying to catch my breath, until the smoke cleared. I ran up the final hill to fight none other than (you guessed it!) Bam-Bam, who was simulating an enemy soldier.

Before starting the course, our instructors had told us, "Never, ever give up your weapon—no matter what."

I knew the football players would try to trick me, but I was determined not to give up my weapon.

When I came face-to-face with Bam-Bam, he said, "There's something wrong with your weapon, new cadet. Give it to me."

I shook my head no.

"New cadet, I *order* you to give me your weapon."

I had been trained to obey orders, and he said there was something wrong with it, so I handed it over.

He banged me upside the head with his pugil stick, threw my weapon all the way back down the hill just to make my life miserable, and said, "Never give up your weapon."

Talk about mind games!

I had to run all the way down the hill, gasping for air, back into the smoke and fire. When I ran back up, of course Bam-Bam was waiting for me.

Again he said, "Give me your weapon."

"Hell no, Bam-Bam—you aren't getting my damn weapon!"

He gave me instructions on how to fight him, and at this point I was so pissed I gave him a good whack or two, until he simply said, "Move on, new cadet."

I got past him and finished the course.

It was horrible being naïve, learning the ropes, being so used to doing what you're told, and listening to people when they gave you orders. But it was good at the same time because we learned to have self-esteem and physical fitness, how to take care of ourselves in precarious one-on-one situations, and how to think and act on our feet.

SETUP FOR SUCCESS AND SERVICE

Through the years, West Point has evolved in how they train cadets. Back when Mark Twain went, there was even worse hazing than I went through. Progressively, it's gotten better and better. Just like society changes, West Point changes along with it. Basic is still there. New cadets still have to learn the four responses, but the methodology is different—instead of trying to weed them out, now it's much more geared toward building them up.

When I went through, training was intense, but they set us up for success once we graduated.

At the end of the first summer, we left our beast company and went to our new, academic year company. Think of a company as a sorority or fraternity house, only military in nature. There were four regiments—first, second, third, and fourth—each with nine companies. I was in the fourth regiment, H company, and we were called The Hogs—no connection to Hogwarts, of course.

We had to meet new friends, new people, and deal with all the upper-class cadets coming back to school. Instead of just the seniors hazing us during Plebe Summer, now we had the sophomores, juniors, *and* seniors, and there was less room to hide. We had to get our books and our schedule. We were in a new rhythm, not doing military training as much as just going to school and focusing on academics.

I carried twenty-three credit hours. We had five-and-a-half days of school, mandatory—we only had to do half days on Saturdays, and we had all day off on Sundays. There were ten to fifteen people in class, so the classes were very small and intimate. It was an excellent education, based on the Thayer method. We were expected to walk into class already knowing the topic and having questions prepared for the professor. To this day, the Thayer method is used to ensure that students are responsible for learning the necessary information. Professors are there solely to clear up any uncertainties, not to lecture.

In class at West Point.

It was a rigorous academic environment. We didn't get to choose our majors until junior year, so we had to take certain classes—like philosophy, calculus, chemistry, English literature, quantum physics, and mechanical engineering—to get a broad education. They wanted us to be well-rounded. And it was a challenge.

At West Point, one of three things is going to get you: the military discipline, the physical education, or the academics. No one gets through with clear sailing. If you're a brainiac, you're going to get your butt kicked in boxing (because of course you have to learn how to box). If you're a fighter from Brooklyn, you may struggle with your academics. If you're a general's son, maybe you didn't want to be there, so you have a problem with discipline.

West Point takes the top 10 percent of high school students and mixes them together, alpha males and females, in an intense environment. What comes out is pretty good—it humbled us and taught us the importance of teamwork, collaboration, time management, and making good decisions. If you ever run into a West Pointer, you're going to get someone reasonably well-rounded, intelligent, and efficient in what they do.

I was an average cadet. I didn't excel at any one thing, but I didn't have any trouble with one thing either. I just went through, enjoying the experience as best I could, learning a lot, and doing as many different things as I could to relieve the tension—things like going to the gym and playing racquetball at night; going on a simple trip to visit the shopping mall in Paramus, New Jersey; or even flying all the way out to Stanford, California, with twenty other cadets to watch West Point play Stanford in football.

These may not sound like a big deal, but we were only allowed to leave West Point two to three times a semester.

Even then, I realized the best was yet to come. West Point was just a precursor to being an officer in the army. There was no doubt I wanted to go through Airborne and Ranger Schools, because that would make me a cut above the typical army officer. It was where the rubber met the road. I knew I was set up to do the best I could because I had the best education and training possible.

Mom and Dad pinning on my second-lieutenant bars.

ARMY SERVICE

After going through Airborne and Ranger Schools, which

I'll tell you more about in a later chapter, I was assigned to the 101st Airborne Division and deployed to Honduras. One of my first missions was to feed the hungry and help the needy in Honduras. It turned into a mission providing protection of values by making sure communism didn't spread in Central America during the time of Daniel Ortega, Nicaragua, and the Sandinistas. The Sandinistas, with the backing of Cuba and the Soviet Union, were trying to spread communism in Central America. The Contras were the various US-backed (and funded) right-wing rebel groups that were active from 1979 to the early 1990s in opposition to the socialist Sandinista junta of Nicaragua. We were deployed to provide support to the Contras.

This was 1983, not that long after the Vietnam War, which had just wound down essentially in 1975. The Sandinista versus Contra conflict wasn't like Iraq or Afghanistan, but it was significant because it was the first time that US soldiers were being deployed close to a combat zone involving proxies of the Soviet Union. Nicaragua was a proxy of the Soviet Union, and Honduras was a proxy of the United States.

During the course of this mission, a soldier in my unit was killed. I can't share the details of what happened, but he lost his life in the line of duty—basically, he was in the wrong place at the wrong time. There was no negligence or anything of that nature, and he hadn't done anything wrong; the loss of life was an unfortunate tragedy.

The passing of this young man was horrible. No one ever wants to lose one of their soldiers, and it made an impact on me—the impact of protecting your men, providing for them, and making sure to avoid conflict and war unless it's absolutely necessary.

Even though "only" one wonderful soldier lost his life, this death taught me the preciousness of life and that everything we read or see glorifying conflict isn't all it's cracked up to be.

I never thought that to begin with. I knew serving in the Army was a serious business. Generally speaking, soldiers do not want to go into combat. Most soldiers are not thinking, "Oh, I can't wait to go to war!" Most realize they are serving their country and hope not to get into conflict—but if we do, they will serve because they signed up to defend and protect the United States and its Constitution.

As the leader of the unit, I had to escort the soldier's body back to Panama, where he would then be escorted back to his hometown for burial and services. The quiet, ninety-minute flight in the helicopter above the Honduran mountain range gave me time to reflect and think through everything that had happened.

After we landed, I sat down and personally wrote what I knew about the soldier.

When soldiers are deployed away from home, they grow together as a team and as friends, so I shared some of that with his family. I talked about how much he meant to our team and our platoon, and I spoke of the effort we were making and the overall situation we were trying to accomplish. He gave his life in the name of the United States, and I wanted his family to know that it wasn't in vain, that we would remember their loved one and show respect for their sacrifice. I promised the family he would never be forgotten, and until the day the mom and dad passed away, I kept in contact with them every year and called or wrote to them on the anniversary of his passing.

In that moment, I was reminded of my time as an altar boy going with the priest to administer funeral rites. I knew that the greatest act of service I could give was being of comfort to people who had lost someone and were grieving.

GOING NUCLEAR

Later in my Army career, I was stationed in Germany where I handled nuclear weapons. During that deployment, East and West Germany were still separated by the Berlin Wall. Soviet troops outnumbered us probably ten to one. We were not at war, of course, but the fear was that the Soviet Union could attack to take over the rest of Europe. Our job was to be more or less a speed bump to slow down the possibility of Soviet tanks and heavy armor crossing the borders to France, West Germany, and the remainder of Western Europe until reinforcements came from the United States.

Somewhere in Germany.

Part of that strategy was to use tactical nuclear weapons that were delivered via cannon artillery. Tactical nuclear weapons are smaller in scale than strategic intercontinental ballistic missiles, but they're very devastating nonetheless. There was never a plan to use the weapons indiscriminately, only if the Warsaw Pact attacked and were making progress across the border. The line in the sand was the Rhine River—if they crossed the river, the plan was to possibly deploy tactical nuclear weapons.

Select units had these nuclear weapons in their inventory—and mine was one of them.

I was a twenty-six-year-old artillery officer, called the nuclear surety officer, for the 3rd Squadron of the 2nd Armored Cavalry. My job was to train my team of officers to determine, if we got a message from Supreme Allied Command Europe (SACEUR), whether it was a valid message to use and deploy nuclear weapons, or whether it was just a test.

Let me explain what this little weapon looks like. Think of a catapult from the Middle Ages: you load the catapult, fire it, and the big mass of concrete hits the castle and starts breaking down its walls. Modern artillery is much more complex. At that point in time, back in 1987, there were weapons that could shoot a one-hundred-pound projectile eight miles within ten meters of where we were trying to get it. Every tactical artillery nuclear weapon I worked with was approximately a hundred-pound projectile.

What separates a regular artillery shell from a nuclear one is something called a permissive action link. Think of a prisoner who has a locked band around their ankle.

It can only be unlocked by the security personnel at the jail. Well, these nuclear weapons have a similar locked band around the projectile. When the permissive action link is locked around this hundred-pound projectile, it can't be loaded into the artillery piece, so it can't be fired.

The president of the United States has an officer walking around with him carrying what's called the football—really a briefcase containing the codes to all the nuclear weapons. In the case of ever deploying a nuclear weapon, the decision goes from the president to the Pentagon to the National Security Agency to the major combatant commanders in Europe, Africa, or wherever we may be. From there, it comes all the way down the unit level—to me.

They regularly did tests with cookies, which are little cards about the size of baseball cards. We would crack the cookie and get a certain code. There were red team cookies and blue team cookies. No one person in America, even today, has both red and blue codes. There are always two people with the codes, and they both have to agree to use them. If they don't, they're not going to be able to unlock the permissive action link and load the nuclear projectile. It's a system of checks and balances for everyone's protection.

When we received a cookie, I'd get a call in the middle of

the night and have to report to the nuclear surety room with my counterparts on the red and blue teams. When we went in, all three of us had loaded pistols. If someone tried to get the code to unlock the permissive action link, we had weapons to stop it, so we wouldn't have a madman with access to nuclear weapons.

After cracking the cookie, there's a long sequence and process of mathematical computations. Ultimately, it would give us a message, either, "This is just a test," or, "This is a live event." Subsequent to that message, our headquarters would send us the actual code either to check the permissive action link, to make sure it was still valid, or to unlock it.

In my job as a captain, I was in charge of the nuclear weapons for our squadron. I had to train the blue team and red team, to make sure they wouldn't crack under pressure or get too nervous. These were young lieutenants who wouldn't know if this was the real thing or not.

Everyone reacts in different ways. I remember one officer getting really nervous and scared. He started to choke up and tremble a little bit. I put my hand on his shoulder and told him, "Don't worry. Everything will be fine. Let's just continue through the sequence." That human touch allowed him to calm down so he felt comfortable and continued with his sequence on the red team while I observed the other officer on the blue team.

The army, and military in general, gives a heck of a lot of responsibility at a young age. Although we weren't actively in a combat situation, being in charge of nuclear weapons is a huge responsibility.

At age twenty, I had just learned how to drive a car—but only one year later, I was a platoon leader in charge of thirty to forty soldiers in Honduras. I was responsible to help lead and serve them in order for these young men to make difficult decisions. A few years after that, the army gave me the responsibility for training of a tactical nuclear weapons surety team within a cavalry squadron in Germany.

Receiving an award from the Supreme Allied Commander Europe (SACEUR).

A LIFETIME OF SERVICE

Serving others at a young age led to a lifetime of service.

After leaving the Army, I continued military service in the National Guard while serving my clients in business, first in the restaurant industry, and ultimately as a financial advisor helping them reach their financial goals.

My experience in the military taught me that to serve people best, I needed an understanding of who they are and where they come from. After I graduated from West Point, I never stopped learning.

CHAPTER 2

Never Stop Learning

One morning at the breakfast table, when I was about ten years old, I asked my mom, "How are babies born?"

The kids in the fourth grade kept talking about the birds and bees, but I didn't understand what they meant. I believed that the stork dropped off the baby, so that explained the birds, but where did the bees come into the mix?

My mom laughed and said, "Wait until after school today. Your father will be home, and we'll both explain it to you then."

It was a funny afternoon. Just as my mom had promised, she and my dad sat me down at the kitchen table. Dad did most of the talking, methodically explaining, using scientific terms, what happened and how it happened. Every once in a while, my mom would add a comment or two and giggle. My dad confirmed some of the street scoop I'd heard from my school and my cousins.

My parents were still young at the time, and although my mom was a little embarrassed, they were happy to help me understand, and the conversation about sex flowed comfortably. It was easy talking to them.

Me and my mom after graduating with a master's degree from Boston University.

RENAISSANCE MAN

Having parents who were so open helped make me

become an open book. I don't filter my thoughts and feelings. They also taught me to never stop learning and experiencing the world around me.

Having different experiences that may sometimes be uncomfortable helps you grow and understand the differences between people. You can still retain your own point of view based on your experiences, but it's important to understand why other people feel the way that they do.

Why do they hold their particular beliefs? It's not a matter of who's right or wrong—it's just different perspectives based on what people have lived through. We don't want to discount other opinions or beliefs; we want to learn why they were formed. If we try to walk in another person's shoes, we may be able to see their point of view.

Everyone deserves to be relevant and heard, unless they're doing something illegal, immoral, or unethical.

We have to want to continue learning and improving ourselves, having the emotional intelligence to know that no one is perfect and there are areas of improvement for each of us. It's important to identify those areas to understand how you are coming across to others and to better present yourself and your point of view in a way that can be understood.

As you'll see in the rest of this chapter, the wide variety of experiences I've had, places I've been, and people I've met have contributed to my lifelong learning.

INTEGRATION EDUCATION

I went to public school during bussing and integration, which was an extraordinarily intense time. There was a lot of upheaval in the country with regards to race relations and the Vietnam War.

For example, my fourth-grade teacher was a very pretty, young black woman named Ms. King. One day, she gave us an assignment to write an essay about Martin Luther King. Of course, we talked to our parents about it, and my dad helped me write my paper.

Unlike most of the other kids, who were very pro-Martin Luther King, I wrote an essay that questioned whether he had done more harm or good for the country. I took the standpoint that he'd done a wonderful job of fighting against injustice, but that his words also caused disturbances and riots.

My father, being a police officer, was called out to help protect and serve when riots and disturbances over the Vietnam War took place. From his law enforcement perspective, unnecessary looting and destruction was directed toward innocent business owners—and many of these businesses were owned and run by black people.

Dad graduating from New York State Trooper Academy.

Compared to the essays the other students wrote, it was a critical piece and unusual for a fourth grader, especially one who had a black teacher. My teacher was exceptionally open-minded regarding the piece but a bit curious about where I received my facts.

I definitely knew a lot about the issues of the time, and grew up with that as a part of my upbringing and heritage. On Sunday mornings as a young boy, my dad and I would watch news shows like *Face the Nation*. I would ask questions, and my father and I would discuss critical events of the day.

These Sunday morning interactions with my dad taught me to keep an open mind. The Martin Luther King essay taught me to think critically and consider different points of view: that of my father, Ms. King, and the essays read out loud by the other students in the class. Nothing is ever black and white—there are many shades of gray.

A decade later, I would have my mind opened again—not on issues of race, but this time about human sexuality.

NORMAN AND ANDY VISIT WEST POINT

As I mentioned in the last chapter, my first summer at West Point was called Plebe Summer. Although I reported on July 5, classes didn't start until after Labor Day. Halfway through the summer, the first week in August, we got a half-day off for visits from family and friends.

In order to have the half-day off, we needed to make sure we didn't have too many demerits, which we'd get for not having our shoes or belt buckles shined, or not knowing how to recite certain memorized facts, which we called "cadet poop"—baloney garbage we had to know off the tops of our heads if we were asked at any point. Instead of saying, "What's the scoop?" we'd say, "Hey, give me the poop!" We had to know the folklore of West Point, the school songs, and plebe knowledge.

For example, when an upperclassman asked us, "What's the definition of leather?" we needed to recite, "If the fresh skin of an animal, cleaned and divested of all hair, fat, and other extraneous matter, be immersed in a dilute solution of tannic acid, a chemical combination ensues; the gelatinous tissue of the skin is converted into a non-putrescible substance, impervious to and insoluble in water; this, sir, is leather."

If we didn't have it right, we got a demerit.

Demerits didn't mean you were really doing anything bad; you just weren't hitting the high standards that were expected. Again, they were trying to teach us to think under pressure while in formation.

I had too many demerits to get the half-day off, which upset me because my mom was going to make the eight-hour trip to see me. Home felt so far away, it might as well have been the moon.

I'm not too proud to say I cried, and it really broke me up because I was so frustrated—I just wanted to see my mom.

My squad leader pulled me into his office and asked, "Carlin, what's wrong?"

"Sir, I've got too many demerits," I explained. "I can't get off this afternoon, but my mom is coming up all the way from Buffalo with some friends. I just wanted to spend a couple of hours with her."

I'll never forget his response: "I totally understand. Don't worry about the demerits; we'll work on that later. You go see your mom."

That was the turning point for me. I needed that comfort right then, and it allowed me to make it through the rest of a rough start. The lesson I learned from my squad leader was compassion, understanding, and flexibility. This is something I had to remind myself of throughout the rest of my life.

THE VISIT

Back in 1978, West Point was pretty much all men. A few females started to attend, but it was primarily an all-male, heterosexual-dominated world.

My mom couldn't drive, and my dad was a police officer and could not get off work, but she didn't want to miss the opportunity to visit, so she got our family friends Andy and Norman to drive her up.

Andy and Norman were friends of the family through my mom's sister. They were great people—and they were homosexual partners. Andy looked like any other man in the seventies, but Norman liked to dress more flamboyantly.

God bless them for driving my mother eight hours to come visit me, but when Norman stepped out of the car at West Point wearing a pink leisure suit, well, I just about wanted to die of embarrassment.

I was so happy to see my mom, and I gave all of them a big hug. But as we walked around West Point, me in my uniform and Norman in his pink suit, he would get excited and scream elatedly when he saw a handsome cadet or officer walk by. I was torn between my gratitude for them driving my mom, not wanting to stand out, and thinking he was pretty funny. It created a new feeling for me—one of loyalty toward a person who was kind to my family, but also an awareness of appearing different. It also gave me a sense of principle, standing by someone and valuing a friendship over what others may have thought. Seeing my mom was an ordinary event, but seeing her in this way, with these friends, was extraordinarily different for the time and place.

My mom brought me my favorite chocolate cake from home in an airtight container. I made sure to share it with my fellow classmates when I got back to the barracks. The visit was very uplifting—it got me through the rest of "Beast Barracks," which is what we called that Plebe Summer, because it's a beast.

Back in 1978, the gay community wasn't as accepted as they are today. Being seen at West Point with my mom and two men wearing pink and green leisure suits taught me that people are people, to respect them for who they are, and to recognize their kindness in bringing my mom up to see me.

Less than ten years later, while in the Army, I saw another symbol of the differences between people get destroyed.

THE FALL OF THE BERLIN WALL

In 1989, my brother Jeff came to visit me when I was

stationed in Germany, and I took leave to go show him the Berlin Wall—on the day it fell.

Prior to that day, in 1987, I had crossed back and forth between East and West Germany while the Wall was still up. We had to go through what was called Checkpoint Charlie, which got its name from the phonetic alphabet back when the wall was first built in the 1960s. There were four occupying powers that could go back and forth with no problem, provided they were in military uniform: the Soviet Union, Great Britain, France, and the United States.

I'd drive up to the checkpoint, which was manned by soldiers from the Soviet Union. Germany was divided in the aftermath of World War II with the eastern portion going to the Soviet Union.

As I'd approach, I'd see warning signs everywhere: "You are entering Soviet-occupied East Germany." The signs also warned people to have out their passports and military IDs and to be in uniform. There was concertina wire, then a space called No-Man's Land, then the actual Wall, which was probably about fifteen feet high, made of rebar and concrete. Soldiers with dogs patrolled the space between the wall and the concertina wire, ready to be let loose on anybody who tried to get over to the other side. It was very stark.

When I'd reach the checkpoint, which was a small guard-house, the guard would come out. He was a Soviet soldier, someone I had been learning how to fight since I'd entered West Point ten years prior. During the first years of my deployment in Germany, the Cold War was still in place between the Soviet Union and the United States.

I'd salute the solider, he'd salute in return, and we'd exchange some pleasantries. This was like two knights tipping their visors at each other in the times of King Arthur. A soldier is still a soldier, even though we were on different sides.

As a peaceful gesture, he wanted to exchange branch insignia, which is a symbol of what part of the Army you're in, worn on your lapel. He was in the Soviet Military Police, and I was US Artillery. We snapped them off of our uniforms and traded them with each other. Then he looked at my papers and gave me the go-ahead to drive into East Berlin.

East Berlin was desolate, just a lot of war memorials and parliamentary buildings that had been used during Wehrmacht Germany and Nazi Germany.

The first time I was there, I went to get my picture taken at a war memorial. I walked up the steps to stand next to a Soviet soldier standing at parade rest with his legs planted a few feet apart. When I got too close, his hand went to his weapon and he moved his foot over the tiniest bit to push a little button that rang a bell and alerted a German paramilitary officer to come and escort me back down the steps.

After that I went to a grocery store off the beaten path, and it was like a third-world store. The shelves were sparse, and the fruit didn't look good. The meat was very plain, and there wasn't much of it. Everything was very gray, very depressed, very dreary.

There weren't many people in East Berlin. A few pedestrians went about their business, and government officials walked by on their way to a government location.

West Berlin was the total opposite, a vibrant city. In East Berlin, women wore skirts down to their ankles and were somewhat frumpy. In West Berlin, women wore miniskirts with high heels. In East Berlin, there wasn't much to do or see, except the historical sites; whereas West Berlin had a main thoroughfare with shopping and plenty of fun things to do. It was a fascinating study of the contrast between communism and capitalism.

THE WALL COMES DOWN

On the day the Berlin Wall came down, throngs of

people—easily forty thousand people or more—clustered around Berlin on both sides of the Wall. Everything was normally very orderly, but that day we knew that something special was going to happening. We were witnessing history.

A guard on the East German side opened the gate by mistake, and the East Germans started coming across. Then the West Germans started coming across, and they saw that nothing bad happened. More and more people went through.

All of a sudden, people started dismantling the Wall, chipping away at it with sledgehammers. My brother and I were right next it, and we were able to get a piece of the Wall that had broken off. To this day, I still have that piece of the Berlin Wall—it represents service and freedom to me.

People were singing, talking, holding hands. Families had been separated for thirty or forty years since the end of World War II. It was huge—so huge, in fact, that it created a migration crisis as many East Germans began migrating to West Germany. The highways were backed up for miles. We had to set up refugee camps to house them as they came west.

It was one of those tremendous moments in the course

of human history. The stars aligned. President Reagan had said, "Mr. Gorbachev, tear down this wall," and they sure did. Amazing.

If you had asked an older European, "Do you think the wall will ever come down?" in their heart of hearts they wouldn't believe it would happen in a million years. That taught me to never say never.

A NEW PERSPECTIVE

These experiences taught me that there are places in the world where, at different times throughout history, people have had a totally different way of life, opposite to mine.

My experiences traveling to China, Russia, Israel, Brazil, and Tanzania have clearly showed me there are many different ways to live. One system may or may not be better than another, but I saw that government is a good thing in some form.

There's a lot we have to be careful about with regard to authority, respect, and higher institutions. We can't just give them a pass, but we do have to realize they serve a purpose to have an orderly, functioning society. Order can be taken too far, but we need some semblance of order because if mankind is left to its own devices, it can be a very bad place indeed.

I did well in the military because I was physically capable and down to earth. Growing up in Buffalo, I experienced a melting pot of people—African American, German, Polish, Irish—instead of growing up insulated in the suburbs. So I was able to talk to and get along with everybody.

We tend to just do what we like or what we're comfortable with. I love walking a mile in others' shoes because then I can better understand them. For example, my experiences with Ms. King, Norman and Andy, and the Soviet soldier at the Berlin Wall highlighted our differences—and our shared humanity.

I recently got back from an HIV clinic where I was able to help others by giving blood. Sitting in the waiting room, I saw what the people who had tested positive for HIV have to go through in order to get healthy—and it opened my eyes. The whole experience got me out of my comfortable routine and, along with other experiences I've shared with you, exposed me to diverse groups of people with different problems and opinions on how the world operates. This way of thinking allows me to see a totally different world.

Being a Renaissance man isn't so much about reading or going to different areas or seeing the arts—though that's part of it—but about going into situations that are uncomfortable, that are a part of our world, and that stretch us.

Another way to learn is by always pushing ourselves to be better—even if we don't always get it right the first time. The next chapter will show you what can be possible if you never give up.

CHAPTER 3

Punch above Your Weight

My dad would always say, "There are all different types of people: there are fishing people, there are camping people, there are mountain people, and there are beach people. We're beach people."

As a young boy at Crystal Beach.

On a beach day, we'd head to Crystal Beach, on the Canadian side of Lake Erie. In the morning, before we'd leave, my mom would fry hamburgers; put ketchup, mustard, and a pickle on them; wrap them in foil; and place them in the picnic basket. Just the smell of them made my mouth water. Whenever we were hungry, we'd grab one—it seemed like there were hundreds of them, because we never ran out.

The three of us kids scrunched together in the back of Dad's 1965 olive green Mustang convertible, with Roxane in the middle on the hump. The top was down, and the wind blew through Mom's hair as she looked over at my dad while he drove. He wore sunglasses and drove with one hand on the wheel and one arm slung casually along the top of the seat next to him. Even though it wasn't a practical family car and it was a tight squeeze in the back seat, I loved riding in the convertible. Mom and Dad made a handsome couple sitting in front, and I knew Dad would play with us at the beach.

When we pulled up, we saw a big, sandy beach that seemed to go on forever. It curved around the lake, leading to the Crystal Beach Amusement Park with a big roller coaster called the Comet—just like the Cyclone at Coney Island. It went close to the water, and from the beach you could see the people screaming by. It was a popular place for families.

Our family would be there all day. Although the days were

often cool at the beginning of summer, by midsummer the temperature soared into the eighties. My brother, Jeff, and I would cool off by playing and splashing in the clear water. Dad came into the water with us, and we played Pickle in the Middle or Keep Away while mom sunbathed on a blanket in the sand.

At lunchtime, we had a picnic then ran along the beach as Dad tossed a football to us. Around four-thirty or five o'clock, we'd all pile back into the car and head home, tired and pink from the sun but happy.

On one such trip, when I was eight years old, my dad walked out into the water and said, "Swim to me."

I took swimming lessons at the local high school, so I was comfortable in the water, and I had practiced paddling around in the lake. I was only about twenty feet away, so I started swimming.

I swam underwater until I tagged him. Then he said, "Good job! Let's try it again."

This time, he stood a little farther away, maybe twenty-five feet, and I swam to him again. When I reached him, he said, "All right! Let's try it one more time."

This time he stood about thirty feet away. I took a big

breath, put my face in the water, and swam and swam and swam. It felt like I was never going to make it; I was getting so tired.

I lifted my head up to take a breath and saw that I was almost there, so I put my head down and kept swimming. Again, it seemed like I was moving and moving but never getting to him. I opened my eyes a little and saw sand being kicked up in the water. Hey! My dad was walking backward, making me swim farther and farther!

I kept going, though. I wanted to prove that I could do it. He kept walking backward, and I kept pushing myself to swim farther and still farther. Finally, when I just about reached my limit, Dad stopped. I pushed through and finally tagged him. He scooped me up, and I was so out of breath, I was just huffing and puffing—but I was victorious!

ALWAYS PUSH HARDER

Swimming with my dad taught me to always try to go a little further, to strive a little harder.

As I grew up, it remained important to me to always push harder, to go to the best schools and always do my personal best. I was determined to do whatever I needed to, in order to put myself in the best position. I was not especially talented or gifted, but I could work hard.

When I wrestled or did judo or studied or went through Ranger School, in the back of my head, I thought, "I have to go above and beyond what's expected of me, in order to get there—and to create luck. Hard work creates good luck."

That work ethic never left me. I realized I was hungry—for success and to provide values for others. Even as a young boy, I knew I couldn't take the easy way out. My parents were always watching. I was compelled to take the harder right instead of the easier wrong.

I was a late bloomer, so I didn't have a lot of distractions. I wasn't interested in girls at a young age, and they weren't really interested in me beyond anything more than a couple little crushes here and there. I could devote more time to my studies, my athletic endeavors, and what I needed to do to get to the next step.

Every stage along my life, I discovered a new step to get me to the next place I wanted to go.

The first step was learning judo, to defend myself when I went to a new school (which I'll tell you about soon). Then I had to get into Canisius High School, to get into the best college I could: West Point.

To get into West Point, I had to keep taking the SAT—I'm

disciplined and a hard worker, but I'm not a very good test taker. I went to the Kaplan school for test prep, I took the test six times to continue to learn how to take it, and I kept improving. Although I wasn't great at standardized tests, I persevered and learned how to do it to get the best possible score. Eventually, I discovered that I could answer questions on the test that I initially hadn't been able to. West Point admired that tenacity. I already had to compensate for my bad eyesight, so showing them that I could keep taking the test and do better each time showed them that if I had to take a hill, even if I got turned back or had to go uphill, I would find a way to take it.

From there, the next step was getting into the best unit I could with the best credentials, Airborne School and Ranger School. I asked myself, "Why just be an officer, when I could be an artillery officer with Airborne and Ranger certification, which would give me credibility when working with infantry and armor units—units that close with and destroy the enemy?"

I continued doing the best I could when I was in the Army. When I decided to leave the military, the next step was to get with the best recruiting firm, which positioned me with the best Fortune 500 company. From there, I learned everything I could about how to be a civilian and a businessman.

When I left that world, I wanted to become a financial

advisor, and I felt Edward Jones would provide me the best training. It required hard work and long hours, but I was able to build my own business through sweat equity, without touching my savings. After becoming a certified financial planner and gaining valuable experience, I became an independent financial advisor with V Wealth Advisors. It was the next logical step in my career. Never stop learning, and always be open to reinventing yourself!

Let me share some of those stories with you.

THE BIG GAME

In late grammar school, the kids in my neighborhood formed football teams and began playing against each other during the summer. It was sandlot football at its greatest.

The teams were divided by geography: the kids on Fordham Street became the Fordham Flyers, the Bedford Avenue kids joined the Bedford Bombers, and I was the captain of the Amherst Astros. Bedford had the most kids, and their team was the perennial powerhouse, but I decided to recruit and train the kids on Amherst Street to finally beat the kids on Bedford and Fordham at football. Finishing last isn't fun.

We recruited and trained Tommy Breyer, who was deaf

and tough as nails. He was like a sledgehammer when he'd go through the line. He took all the punishment the other team doled out—and he gave it right back. He ran the football with reckless abandon, hitting people as he went. Then I recruited Mickey Stanley. We called him The Cougar because he was very fast, and when he ran the ball, he'd roar like a cougar. We also had Sam Speciale. He was a very good athlete, very talented—fast and skilled with the ball. He was our best player. My brother, Jeff, played, of course, and his nickname was Cannonball because he ran low to the ground and would knock people over. I was the quarterback and coach. There were some other kids involved, but these were the key players.

Reliving "Cannonball up the middle" fifteen years later.

Prior to the start of the football season, I began studying how football teams prepare, and I'd use those drills. One was the Oklahoma nutcracker drill, which involved two linemen blocking and a running back having to get through. They were very physical drills. We would also do some conditioning drills, like what Crossfit does today but without the weights. We did burpees and jumping jacks and mountain climbers to get our stamina up. It was like a mini-training camp. For little kids, it was kind of fun—but it was very structured and organized.

We'd go to the big grassy area in front of Public School 64 and play two or three games against each team throughout the summer. The first season, when I was ten, we lost practically all the games. The next year, we broke even. The third year, at age twelve, we won all the games up to the championship, where we faced the previously undefeated Bedford Bombers.

We played hard, but we were down near the end of the game. For the last play, we were on the goal line with only a second left. We went into the huddle, and I looked at everybody—all the kids were there looking at me, sweaty and dirty—and said, "Gentlemen, we're going to score. Cannonball up the middle."

Everyone nodded, clapped their hands, and we broke the huddle. We all knew what we had to do.

The play went off exactly as I planned: I handed Jeff the ball, he burst through the defensive line, and we scored the winning touchdown. We would not be denied, after all the training and practice. It was a really big moment because we saw the mantle of "the best and the toughest" go from Bedford to the Amherst Astros.

After the game, I had my teammates invite their parents to an awards banquet the following week at the Broadway Grill, a train caboose turned into a nice restaurant, which was the neighborhood joint where everyone went to dinner. All the kids came with their parents.

I talked about how hard we had worked for the last three years and how everyone contributed. Jeff and I made up little playbooks as awards for next season—I was already preparing for next year—with different honors like Most Valuable Player, Most Improved Player, Best Specialty Player. I made sure everyone got some type of award, and all the parents clapped.

It was such a fun thing, so innocent, not costly and not that extravagant. People couldn't wait until the next year to do it all over again.

As it turned out, however, we started going in different directions after that. We would still get together every so often, but it was different as we all started high school.

Looking back, it was like that movie *Stand by Me* or *The Sandlot*. It was that time period when things were just simpler. When we played, there were never really any parents around. If there was a disagreement, the kids would settle it.

After games, we would go to Mesmer's Dairy and order orange Zing to drink. Then we'd get some Slim Jims, Swee-Tarts, and chips. We would sit on the ledge of the school by the big trees or lie on the grass to talk. We'd buy some Topps football cards to trade while we ate our little picnic as the sun was going down and the shadows grew longer.

Those were the days—and they set me up for more experiences with team sports as I got older.

FROM CUT TO CHAMP

The Canisius High School football team was a powerhouse. I had watched them win sixty straight games when I was a kid, and it was my dream to play for them.

Prior to my freshman year, the coach sent out a card to all the new kids, asking them to try out for the football team. Mine said, "Be great in '78," and handwritten by the coach himself was the message, "Be sure to try out for the team!"

I was so excited to try out. I'd never played anything more

organized than the games I arranged with the neighborhood kids, but I was a good athlete and I thought I was pretty good at football. The problem was that I was also really small—I'm talking ninety pounds, soaking wet, my first year of high school.

Still, I tried out for the team and did my absolute best. We all practiced together for a week, and then there was the first round of cuts—and my name was called. I was so bummed, but I accepted it and said I'd try again next year.

I put my emphasis on continuing to train for judo, which I'll tell you more about in a later chapter. That first year at Canisius, I didn't play any sports for the school, but I was winning judo tournaments, getting better, and earning my brown belt—just one belt away from a black belt.

When sophomore year came along, I said, "I'm going to make the team this year!" I worked on my speed and strength. When I came back from summer break, I was 105 pounds. I thought for sure that those added fifteen pounds would make all the difference. I was little, but I was fast.

The problem was that none of the coaches knew me. The other kids had either played last year or spent the summer playing summer league with the coaches. I hadn't done that, so I got cut again.

I knew that I definitely wanted to participate in some type of sport for the school, so it was time to turn my attention to something new. I decided to try cross-country because I liked running. I also knew I was going to go out for the wrestling team later that year, so that would keep me in really good shape.

I joined Coach Skipper's cross-country team. I was small and somewhat muscular—not tall with long, lean legs for running fast and far—so I was an average runner, but I always kept plugging along, which is the secret to cross-country running. At our meets, Coach Skipper urged us to run harder, catch up to the next guy, and keep moving. I liked that he pushed me on. Ultimately, I earned a JV letter in cross-country.

TO THE MAT

In November, when I got to wrestling practice, I was in wonderful shape from all that running, so the wrestling conditioning was very easy.

I backed off my judo practice a little bit because I couldn't do both practices. But what I'd learned from judo helped me be a good wrestler. The two are similar; judo is basically Japanese wrestling with throws, arm bars, and chokeholds.

My first wrestling match was against Kevin Kimball, the previous year's champion at the eighty-eight-pound weight class. That year, we were both wrestling at ninety-eight pounds. At the time, I didn't know anything about Kevin Kimball, and my more senior teammates didn't say anything to me about him. I didn't think anything of going up against such a good wrestler; I just exuded confidence. I knew I had stamina and that I was going to throw this guy and pin him.

My match was third. It was at Bishop Neumann High School, an away match, so we didn't have many people there cheering for us. When we came out to warm up, the song "Sir Duke," Stevie Wonder's loving tribute to Duke Ellington, was playing, and it was pretty cool knowing that I was going to get to compete.

When my match was called, I went out, shook hands with Kevin Kimball, and immediately threw him. He didn't know who I was; he just thought I was easy prey. But nobody else had judo experience, so he'd never wrestled somebody with those skills. I threw him, put him on his back and, amazingly, I pinned him.

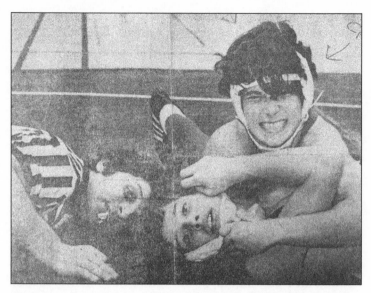

Sophomore year, I was a ninety-eight-pound weakling.

He never got up. Our whole team jumped up and cheered for me. I felt amazing. They thought I came out of nowhere—some of these kids had wrestled for four years, and here I'd just pinned last year's champion in the first forty-five seconds, in my very first match.

I was a superstar.

I even got my picture in the newspaper, the *Buffalo News*. That lit my wrestling career on fire at Canisius. All of a sudden, I got so much respect—it didn't even matter that I'd gotten cut from football.

Coach Emery Rogers says, "Never put your head down."

In fact, after I placed in the All-Catholic Championships and got into the high school Hall of Fame, the football coach who had cut me, Coach Jeff Gemmer, said, "Hey, Carlin, I want you to know that I'm taking credit for your wrestling wins. If I hadn't cut you, you wouldn't have taken the passion you had for football and turned it into wrestling."

Harry Potter on top of the podium.

To this day, we keep in touch as friends. I always call him Coach even though he never actually coached me. He even came with me to the Army West Point/University of Buffalo game and met all my Army buddies. We had a wonderful time—me and the football coach who cut me from the team.

Just think: if I'd never been cut from the football team, I'd never have had that great wrestling career—which went on to help me get into West Point, setting me on a great track for the rest of my life.

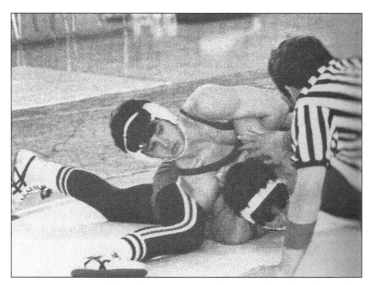

Easy does it!

RANGERS LEAD THE WAY

I went to West Point to learn how to be a soldier. After graduation, cadets select which branch of the US Army they want to join: infantry, armor, artillery, etc. Just think of it as a civilian school where you're going into residency or apprenticeship after you graduate to be a doctor, an attorney, an engineer, or an architect.

I went to Fort Benning, Georgia, for a month to become a paratrooper, then followed that with Canadian jump school in Edmonton, Alberta. After Airborne school, I went to field artillery officer basic training at Fort Sill, Oklahoma.

Then I signed up for Ranger School. Army Rangers are an elite force similar to Navy SEALs.

I had to apply to get accepted. They only take the best in the class. Most field artillerymen don't go to Ranger School—but I wasn't the average field artilleryman. I wanted to punch above my weight and make sure that I knew everything I could about small-unit tactics, infantry, leadership, and decision-making under duress, so I specifically requested to go to Ranger School. I competed and was selected.

As a West Pointer, going to Ranger School is like being valedictorian or graduating with honors from a civilian college. The Ranger tab is a recognized tab of excellence in the US Army, so we wore it on our uniforms above our unit patch on our left shoulders, and everyone knew that we'd successfully graduated from Ranger School; it's a big deal.

One day, years later, my wife and I were watching a Discovery Channel special on Ranger School. Forty-five minutes into the show, she asked, "Is that what you did?" I replied, yes. After ten years of being married, she said, "You're a badass!"

Well, I may not be a badass, but I did go through some experiences that the average person probably hasn't been through.

LEARNING THE ROPES

I had a thirty-day vacation before I had to report to Ranger School. I needed to know how to tie fourteen different knots within a certain length of time, but I had no experience with that either, so while home on vacation, I looked up a mountain climber to teach me the ropes.

My dad, who always supported me and my service, was a great teaser. He would come downstairs while I was with the mountain climber and ask, "What are you doing?"

I said, "You know, I'm learning how to tie knots. I'm paying Joe here to teach me so I'm ready for Ranger School."

He said, "But you're on vacation."

I said, "I know, but I really need to learn this because they're going to test me, and it's one less thing I have to worry about, so it will give me confidence going into school."

It was funny because my dad was making fun of me about learning ropes during my vacation, but that's kind of the way I was. I always wanted to try to be the best I could. And to be the best at what you're trying to do, you have to go above what the normal person does.

I ended up passing the ropes with flying colors. I needed

to get twelve out of fourteen to go on to the next phase—and I got thirteen, which was fantastic.

I also studied the manuals on patrols, ambushes, and raids. I wanted to be able to give the right orders at the right time to the right people, without hesitation.

Ranger School in the winter of 1983 was a nine-week intensive training in commando-style tactics of reconnaissance, raids, and ambushes. Reconnaissance missions are to look and watch and see what's going on without being detected. Ambushes are where Rangers get information on the enemy in order to ambush and kill them. Raids are when Rangers surprise the enemy when they're somewhat stationary and kill them or rescue somebody. When the Grenada Operation occurred, Rangers were the ones who went in and rescued the medical students who were being held by the Cubans in Grenada. In the Normandy Invasion, US Army Rangers were some of the first to hit the beach.

The first three weeks at Ranger School were to weed out the people who weren't physically tough enough. The next three weeks involved training in a mountainous area. Then, the last three weeks involved training in a jungle and wetlands area. We had to walk through the Everglades, at times with water that would be over our heads, and we had to get to an island, attack it, and then cross back over to the mainland on military rafts. They wanted to teach us how to operate in the jungle, in the mountains, and in areas surrounded by water.

We had to pass different tests in each phase, such as a land navigation test and a rope-tying test. We had to pass patrols that involved intensive team planning and execution. They taught us how to operate with lack of food, lack of sleep, and under intense physical duress.

I knew when to deploy the machine gunners to the left and the right; I knew when to set off a star cluster to begin the attack and when I was going to bring up the rear detachment. I knew sequentially, if A happens, I do step one. If B happens, I do step two. If C happens, step three. I had to not only think this way but learn to think sequentially under duress because while all these steps are happening, there's also an enemy who has a vote. I couldn't hesitate. I had to know what to do and when to do it.

WHERE'S THE BEEF?

We were only supposed to eat when the Ranger School cadre allowed us to—but it wasn't just to be strict. There's a good reason for this rule: when you're under duress and not eating a lot, you can smell things from a long way away. It's also a matter of discipline, and it kept us focused.

We had C-rations, which were cans of food, and a P-38 to open it. The P-38 is a little can opener that fits between your forefinger and thumb and attaches to your dog tags. It's called that because you had to turn it thirty-eight times to open the lid on your food. We would wrap the cans of food in socks and put them in our packs wherever we had room so we'd have them as we were patrolling deep in the woods.

One day, we were marching in the mountains, and I was darn hungry. We weren't supposed to eat yet, but I was able to surreptitiously open a can of potatoes and beef. The potatoes were on top with little circular patties of beef, kind of like sausage, about half an inch thick on the bottom of the can. I ate it cold, no problem—and at the time, it was delicious.

Suddenly, the cadre leader stopped the patrol. "Rangers, halt."

We all stopped in our tracks, standing in our patrol caps as the sun started to go down.

He barked, "Who's eating?"

He had smelled the food.

I held my lips shut, making sure this guy couldn't smell

anything coming out of my mouth—he would kick my butt, literally and figuratively.

"Rangers, who is mother-effing eating?"

Our leader was so pissed. If he caught me breaking the rules, he'd give me a demerit sheet. Then I'd have to dig a six-by-six-foot hole to bury that sheet. I was already tired—exhausted, really—and still so hungry. There was no way in hell I wanted to get a demerit sheet on top of it.

He walked up and down the line looking at us. He could tell the general area he smelled food, and he came to a stop in front of the guy I was standing next to, a bigger guy.

The leader leaned up and smelled the guy's face to see who the hell was eating. I didn't breathe for a second. I had the can behind my back, pushed up against my butt, and I just kept my mouth shut and looked down. I tried not to stand out. I wasn't the biggest or the smallest; I was just average-looking, so I usually blended in pretty well. Sometimes it helps to be ordinary!

It seemed like an eternity that I stood there, mouth clamped shut, too afraid to even breathe through my nose.

Finally he gave up trying to figure out who it was, but he

warned us that there'd be hell to pay if he caught anyone eating.

I dodged a big bullet there—and I lived another day, to push even harder and eat even faster!

GRADUATING WITH HONORS

At Ranger School, my classmates were just what I had expected: young men with long, distinguished lineages in the military, the sons of West Pointers and generals. One of my classmates was the grandson of General Creighton Abrams, who served in Patton's army.

Ranger Carlin, second row, tenth from the right.

General Abrams was the lead battalion commander at the Battle of the Bulge in World War II. Abrams later served as a general in the Vietnam War and was appointed Chief of Staff of the Army. The Abrams tank is named after him. And his grandson, Abe Abrams, was in Ranger School with me.

If you were taking bets in Vegas on who would be the honor grad—Abe Abrams, the grandson of General Abrams, or Tim Carlin from Buffalo, who never even served a day in the Boy Scouts—you'd probably take Abe. In April 1983, however, four men graduated with top honors—General Abrams's grandson wasn't one of them, but I was!

Receiving top honors in Ranger School meant leading men from good military families who really wanted to serve. They all had strong personalities, we were all sleep-deprived and thrust into difficult environments, out in the woods or the Everglades, in water, or in the desert. We had to lead patrols of ten to a hundred men.

I was in Ranger School because I wanted to be an elite officer, and Ranger School gave me that capability. I definitely punched above my weight there, because of the 150 people who started Ranger School with me, only fifty-three graduated.

So it was a big deal for me to be one of the honor graduates—one of the top four of those fifty-three. That's
a pretty cool thing—and I wouldn't have been there
if I hadn't prepared myself through learning judo as a
picked-on kid, then wrestling, then West Point.

Frankly, before my military training I didn't know my butt
from a hole in the wall about surviving in the wilderness.
I was a city boy. The closest I'd gotten to camping out in
Buffalo, New York, was lying on the grass at Public School
64 and talking with my buddies until the streetlights
came on.

I was really proud to be an honor graduate because it
indicated that I knew how to build a team and utilize
that team to get a job done.

YOU CAN ALWAYS GIVE A LITTLE MORE

Why do some people fail and others rise to the occasion
under duress?

Throughout my life leading up to that point, my strength
was my ability to think clearly in tough situations, even in
the midst of chaos. I have an ability to size up a situation
and give direction to people. When I give direction—
whether in the military, in the restaurant industry, or
with my clients now—I give it with conviction and have

confidence in what I'm saying. You have to commit. To be a leader you can't be wishy-washy. People who work with me like that I have conviction and they get proactive direction.

That's what Ranger School taught me. That's what West Point taught me. That's what the Army, and PepsiCo, and all these great firms I've been with have taught me. Ranger School made me a better Army officer. As I said, I went through it because I wanted to serve in the best way possible, and I felt that the more exposure I got to training, the better I would be.

That training helped me later, too, in my civilian jobs. When I first started my financial services career, which I'll tell you more about in an upcoming chapter, I worked seven days, eighty hours a week, which is at least as much as I worked at Ranger School. Building a business means helping the clients when they need you—*whenever* they need you. If they called at any hour, it was ingrained in me to serve them and be there. If someone needed an appointment on a Saturday night or Sunday, they would get it.

I remember one time I helped a client who only had time to meet with me on Saturday nights because he was an entrepreneur. We met at eleven o'clock at night and stayed until one in the morning. Another client was a soldier stationed at Fort Riley who wanted to invest about fifty dollars a month with me. One Saturday afternoon, I hopped in the car and drove three hours during a snowstorm down to Fort Riley, spent three or four hours explaining everything to him, and then drove back. I don't say this to toot my own horn; I just want to highlight the extra effort that West Point, Ranger School, and the military teach you to give. Even when you think you're fatigued and done, you still have 40 to 50 percent left.

NEVER GIVE UP

When I was small and realized that I wasn't going to be a football player, I had to ask myself, "How can I be the best wrestler for my weight class?"

How could I take that frustration and anger—about being too short, too small, legally blind—and turn it around? By focusing it and channeling it into success. By not taking the easy way out and always pushing harder. By punching above my weight and believing in myself.

When you set goals, you should set them so high that you barely feel you can achieve them. That way, if you don't quite achieve them, you know that they were so aggressive and high that you won't even be upset—you'll just have something else to strive for next time.

In fact, you may even come to see failure as good. I have learned more through failing than I have through succeeding. We become better and more complete by failing.

At the same time, though, you don't want to give up when things are difficult or when you don't get it right the first time.

It's important to keep going, to keep seeing things positively, and to find a way to improve your life. You may not get it to 100 percent, but even 10 or 20 percent can make a difference. You can redefine what success looks like. If you're always trying to make incremental improvements in every area of your life, even if it's only 1 percent, if you never give up and keep pushing a little bit more and more, you discover new things along the way: new experiences, insights from new people you meet, or even discovering a new food that you like—things you maybe otherwise wouldn't have had the chance to experience.

There's always more to learn and do and more ways to grow and evolve. It's exciting. You don't grow old if you're doing that. If you're always learning, you're not slowing down.

In the words of Dory from *Finding Nemo*, "Just keep swimming!" Just like I did when I was a kid swimming toward my dad in Lake Erie.

CHAPTER 4

Never Stand Still

In 1996, I was working for PepsiCo as the director of franchise operations when I was transferred to Tulsa, Oklahoma, to help Kentucky Fried Chicken franchises grow their businesses and the KFC brand in Oklahoma, Kansas, and Texas.

I wasn't much of a dancer, but moving out West I knew I had to learn how to country western two-step because all the ladies in Oklahoma danced like that.

I found an Arthur Murray Dance Studio and a wonderful teacher named Donna Beth Shrader. I put myself out there and learned how to dance. I got pretty good at it. I enjoyed the music; it made me happy and relaxed after long days at work—and dancing was great exercise too.

One day, Donna Beth said, "You're getting really good at this country western two-step. Would you like to learn some new dances?"

"Like what?" I asked.

"Well," she said, "you can learn salsa, tango, foxtrot, waltz, rumba, cha-cha, bolero—all the different ballroom dances."

"Sure, let's do it!"

I kept learning, and I kept dancing.

Eventually, I was having so much fun, I even began to enter some small competitions and showcases, demonstrating the dances in front of an audience. I just kept getting better and better.

In 2000, I took a position in Chicago as a national restaurant consultant. That's where I met my friend Jack Winerock, who was an attorney working for the city. He was about twenty years my senior and took a shine to me.

Me, Dad, and Mom at a pub inside the Chicago Loop.

As a lifelong Chicagoan, Jack showed me the city inside and out—the different neighborhoods, independent food restaurants, dance clubs and places to meet single ladies, and speakeasies that operated during Prohibition and were now cool, funky joints. He also taught me different ways of getting around traffic, when to use public transportation, and when not to.

After the 2001 downturn and recession hit, I got laid off, and fortunately I had some money saved for a rainy day. One day, sitting in Jack's apartment overlooking downtown Chicago and musing about life, Jack saw an advertisement for professional single men who knew how to dance to be gentlemen hosts onboard the *Queen Eliz-*

abeth II. These gentlemen hosts would dance with single ladies who wanted to dance but didn't have an escort or married ladies whose husbands didn't want to dance—just like in the movie *Out to Sea* with Jack Lemmon and Tony Curtis. If you haven't seen the movie, it's a hilarious comedy about being a gentleman host onboard a cruise ship and meeting eligible ladies. One of my favorite scenes is when the two main characters are in their cabin, arguing about getting the first dance with a pretty girl. They end up falling out of the bunk beds and knocking themselves out, so they miss the dance altogether.

I had to go out to Oak Brook, in the suburbs of Chicago, for two interviews: the first was a dance interview, to make sure I knew how to dance, and the second was an interview to make sure I had good manners and proper diction. The passengers on this high-end around-the-world cruise paid anywhere from $60,000 to $100,000 for the experience, so they wanted someone sharp.

"I'd love to see the world," I said during my interview.

"You will," the interviewer told me. "And the ladies will love you because you're so young. Typically, our gentleman hosts are retired men."

I passed both interviews and was hired to do a test run on a short seven-day Mediterranean cruise in September.

Everything was paid for, even my own passenger stateroom. I flew to London and boarded the *Queen Elizabeth II* at the harbor (or harbour, as it's spelled in the UK). The cruise visited Barcelona, Lisbon, Rome, and Paris.

When I returned from that cruise, they said I had done a great job and asked me to join the around-the-world cruise, which stopped in thirty-six ports touching every continent around the world, with a duration of three-and-a-half months. The cruise would begin in New York City in January and conclude in April, back in New York City.

Gentleman host onboard the Queen Elizabeth II.

"Twist my arm," I told them. I'll tell you about that amazing adventure later in this chapter. But first, an excursion into romance.

"CAN YOU DANCE?"

I learned early in life not to be afraid to ask for what I want, to make myself heard.

My mom had a big personality. Her role model growing up was Marilyn Monroe, and she looked like a blonde Betty Boop. When Mom walked into a room, she made an impression—and she made sure she was noticed. She also had amazing energy, drive, and competitive spirit. Because of her, I had an upbringing that emphasized not being afraid to make a splash. She gave me tremendous confidence that set the groundwork for me to try new things. She had a spirit that I embraced and learned from.

Because of that energy—never standing still, always trying to improve and learn new things—I was somewhat fearless. When I met my wife, she detected that confidence and fearlessness in me, and she liked that.

On December 20, 2002, two weeks before I was supposed to leave for the cruise, I attended a big dance party in downtown Chicago. All the dance studios brought their students to dance the night away, and before the dancing started, an instructor gave lessons on the floor.

From across the room, a tall blonde wearing black pants and a red sweater caught my eye as she moved. Immediately, I thought, "I have to meet her."

At this party, in order to meet new people and so every-body got a chance to dance, the instructors would teach a move and then everybody would partner up. The women stood in a big circle, facing in, and the guys stood inside that circle, facing the girls. I strategically positioned myself one person to the left of the blonde woman so that as soon as we switched partners, I'd have the opportunity to dance with her.

I positioned myself assuming we'd move clockwise, but unfortunately the circle of men moved counterclockwise, so it would take an entire hour of dancing with other part-ners and making polite conversation with those women before my turn to dance with this beautiful blonde came around. "I blew it," I thought. Surely another gentleman would make good conversation and catch her interest before I could.

An hour later, I was finally in position. "I'm Karen," she said.

"I'm Tim." I smiled as I looked at her. "Can you dance?" I asked teasingly.

She looked back at me, straight into my eyes, and said, "If I have a good leader."

We didn't say anything else to each other, but I was

determined to show her I was a good leader in all these different dances—we moved through the rumba, foxtrot, waltz, and cha-cha.

Each dance has a different feeling, rhythm, and emotional state you go into as you move together. When we did the cha-cha, it was very flirty. The waltz is extremely romantic and graceful. Doing a tango is an argument between a man and a woman deeply in love. With each dance we had together, it was like we were a different couple: flirty, romantic, sexy, graceful, in love, a couple arguing.

You can learn a lot about a person by how you lead and follow in these different ballroom dances—all without saying a word.

As we floated across the floor doing all these different dances, it was a magical moment. We were as intimate as could be while being fully clothed—her touch, being different characters, expressing different aspects of our personalities, physically, to music. Moving and connecting together is extremely powerful.

It was at that moment, through the power of dance, that we both fell in love with each other.

We had each come with different friends to the dance. We apologized to them and said we were going to go salsa dancing at another club in downtown Chicago—more flirty fun.

The dance party ended around eleven o'clock, and we danced at Nacional 27, a salsa club on Huron Street, until after one in the morning. After that, we ended up back in my apartment in downtown Chicago, right off the river.

We ordered Chinese food, and then we sat and talked the rest of the night and through the morning. We shared our hopes, our dreams, and our fears.

I learned that Karen was thirty-five and had never been married. She worked for a lawyer and had a cat named Holly. She was the opposite of the women I had dated previously: she was shy, quiet, and introverted, but she was also loyal, honest, and faithful. I knew right away, in my gut, that I could trust her. We talked very deeply and openly with no hidden agenda or fear of putting ourselves out there. We talked about family, children, sex, money, religion, and, yes, even politics!

Karen didn't have a college degree, but she was smart and had acquired a great business sense through her years of work as a legal secretary. She was good at taking care of herself and had no debt.

We were completely honest with each other. We weren't kids anymore; we'd met each other at the perfect time in our lives—we were both old enough to know what we wanted and smart enough to realize we had found it in each other.

Finally, around six-thirty the next night, Karen had to go home to take care of her cat. I cleaned up the house a bit and freshened up. I realized, even in that short time, I already missed her—that's when I knew I was hooked.

The next day, we went out and I met her mom and family. I think they liked me, and they could tell just by looking at Karen that something big was happening.

On the third day, I took her to dinner at Petterinos, an Italian restaurant inside the Loop of downtown Chicago.

Earlier that day, I had called my mom and told her I wasn't going to make it home for Christmas after all.

"What's wrong? Did something happen?" she asked.

"Yes, something happened—something wonderful! I met a girl. She's the *one*, Mom. I just met her, but I can tell she is the one."

It was a few days before Christmas, and it was snow-ing. The restaurant was warm and romantic, and Karen looked beautiful.

After having met a number of different ladies, I realized that Karen was a great partner for me. She's trusting, loyal, graceful, and very intelligent. I didn't want to miss a moment with her, so I proposed precisely seventy-two hours from the moment we first met. And she immediately said yes, adding, "It'll never be boring!"

Later, Karen called her dad to announce that we were engaged. He replied, "That's wonderful! I'm very happy for you. Tell me about Tim." Karen told him a few sentences, and then—in his low-key way—he asked, "What else is going on?" He just wasn't concerned—he had been in the Army in the 1950s, so there was a certain degree of trust and comfort for him knowing that his daughter was marrying a fellow Army man.

In fact, all of Karen's family was very happy for us. They had scratched their heads for years, wondering how in the world Karen wasn't already married. Finally, all the pieces were falling into place.

There was, however, one hiccup to getting engaged and married: I was leaving soon for the around-the-world cruise. I was already committed to going, and Karen— being a dancer and travel-lover—understood completely.

If the roles had been reversed, she would have wanted to go. I promised to find her the perfect ring while I was on my travels, and she said she would plan the wedding while I was gone.

It was a big step. When I left on the trip, we'd only known each other for two weeks, but there was a lot of trust. Two weeks after proposing, early one Saturday morning, Karen brought me to Chicago O'Hare airport and slowly walked me to the gate. With a tear in her eye, she kissed me goodbye, and I left to sail around the world.

AROUND THE WORLD

While I was on the cruise, I kept a journal, writing about where we went, what was happening on the ship. Every day, I also wrote to Karen by email. "Hey, we just stopped in Japan. About 250 Japanese people came onboard. We're going to see Nagasaki today, where the bomb went off."

Some of my younger dance partners onboard the Queen Elizabeth II.

The end of the cruise was right before the invasion of Iraq, so sometimes that made its way into our letters. "There's been a lot of talk about going to war with Iraq because of everything that's been on TV. There's a buzz about the ship."

"Hey, by the way, there's a diva onboard the ship, taking over."

FROM: Tim Carlin

TO: Karen Gecas

SENT: February 1, 2003 9:00 AM

Dear Sweetheart,

I love you and miss you very much. I visited the onboard tour office to see if there were any openings. They sent a message to New Zealand and I should hear something Monday so keep your fingers crossed.

On the invitation I think my name goes first then Lieutenant Colonel then United States Army, but I could be wrong. Maybe United States Army is abbreviated and goes in parenthesis after the rank (USA). It just didn't look right the other way around. If there is a question, you can call Jose Davis and he can better advise. Jose is a protocol officer who we will invite to the wedding with his wife, Candice. Let me know what you find out.

I'm open to going informal later in the day for dinner but not too informal. I think we should be dressed elegant informal at the very least. I do not want jeans or shorts. Maybe cocktail dresses for ladies and open-collar shirts and sport jackets for the men. I like the idea of outdoor dancing and a formal dinner, providing the bugs stay away and it's not too hot.

Today we cross the International Date Line. We lose February 2nd and go right to the third. When proceeding east from Greenwich, England, one hour is lost for every 15 percent of longitude. When proceeding west from Greenwich, one hour is gained for every 15 percent of longitude. Consequently, 360 degrees divided by 15 degrees equals 24 hours, which causes one day to be lost when circumnavigating the globe eastwards and one day to be gained when circumnavigating the globe westwards. To compensate for the difference, one day is added when crossing the International Date Line going east and one day is subtracted when going west. Consequently, Sunday, February 2nd does not exist and local time onboard ship is Greenwich Mean Time +13.

I have some pictures I am sending you once I get to Auckland, New Zealand. I have a picture of me and a passenger with two gentlemen hosts onboard the ship as we sail away from Moorea (Bali Hai). Then I have me going to the stingray tour with the QE2 in the background. Next is a shot of me and the Moorean boat driver. Then a picture of me and the guide with the giant stingrays. Look how big they are! Then I have a picture of me taking a photograph of the room onboard the QE2. Next is the King Neptune celebration when we crossed the equator. Then a picture of the Pacific dream party with Lillian, an 82-year-old "hottie." She is a wonderful dancer and would put many 22 year olds to shame. Then a picture of a flower that I had another dream about. I'll cover that in my next email. On Tahiti, we went to the botanical gardens and I took a picture of Tim petting Timmy the turtle. Look how big he is. Then I enclosed two pictures of the Tahitian countryside and the picturesque waterfalls.

Today we have a port lecture on the city of Auckland. It lasts an hour and gives a good overview of the history and culture of the city. It also provides information on what to do and where to go in Auckland. Yesterday, I saw a movie on an oil rig in the North Atlantic. The company portrayed was Phillips 66 Company, my old company I worked for in Tulsa, Oklahoma. That was a pleasant surprise. The Captain of the ship wrote a book called *The QE2,* and I had a copy given to me today. Later in the voyage I'll have him sign the book and it'll be a great keepsake. The exchange rate is 1.70 to one U.S. dollar in New Zealand. It might be a good place to buy a diamond. :)

How are you feeling? I know you are busy and have plenty to do with the wedding and work, but are you feeling happy? I hope you are. The emails are fun, aren't they? I wait with anticipation every day to hear from you. I feel like a little boy waiting for a Cracker Jack toy in the mail out in the middle of Kansas. Honey, why is the 6th of May such an important day to be married? I like the date, but you have such an affinity for it and I wonder why?

I was invited to a little cabin party last night by a couple from Chicago. He is a retired United Airlines pilot on the world cruise, and we had fun. There were 8 people there and it lasted for about an hour. It's like a little family onboard amongst all the world cruise travelers. We sat on two single beds facing each other, drinking red wine and passing around cheese and crackers. I thought of you and our future. I imagined us entertaining our friends and hugging each other on the bed while laughing, telling the story of how we met and then romanced each other for months halfway around the world through email. I love you and miss you.

Love you spoon buddy,

Tim

* * *

FROM: Karen Gecas

TO: Queen Elizabeth 2

SENT: February 7, 2003 7:23 PM

SUBJECT: Tim Carlin, Room 4241

Hello My Love,

Well, you were busy at the computer the other day—it must have taken you a good while to type those two letters! I have to say that that was a pretty unique dream you had—thanks for sharing it with me, although the reference of "dirty blonde" grass isn't so appealing. I think the more appropriate term to use is dishwater blonde...I'll let you slide this time. :) So you were mesmerized by the sheep and took a full roll of film. Wow...those must have been some pretty interesting sheep...either that or you have a very strange fetish! (Don't worry, I'm not thinking the latter.) The blowing of the horns...I've always thought it interesting watching those little tugboats move the ship away from the dock. I wish I could have been there next to you waving goodbye... although I would have actually been with the others on land waving another sad goodbye.

I've forwarded your letter. Jose Davis replied to me that he is a good friend of yours—or so he thought—since he found out secondhand that you are to be married. He was kidding and congratulated us on our upcoming wedding. Art Kovach also replied with a congratulations.

Not much to report since my last email. Tonight I was supposed to go with Gil, Tamara & Carolyn to the TGIF dance party, but I decided to take a pass. I've been tired all week and especially this afternoon—I've been doing nothing but yawning, so once I get out of here I'll have a nice quiet evening at home. Tomorrow I have class and then at some point will be at Kim's for Kenny's b'day. I may also hook up with Lisa for a drink.

I was getting together a couple of checks of yours to deposit and I realized that the stamps you gave me are old. They're $0.34 and we now use $0.37 so I'll have to get some 3-cent stamps—I hope the previous deposits made it! I'm mailing in the reorder form for more deposit slips—wasn't sure if you would actually need them but figured it's better to have extra than not enough. You also received another Southwest Companion Pass so I filled that out too for mailing. The pass you sent in for before leaving has already come in. RCI sent a notice indicating that your deposited vacation week (The Pines at Treetop Condominiums) will expire on 6/30/03. It mentions that for $49 you can purchase an RCI Guest Certificate so someone can go in your place.

Well that's all for now. I love you very much and look forward to spending the rest of our lives together. Oh...in your letter I forwarded, I like the part where you indicate that your real job in Armenia will be to travel around Eastern Europe visiting strange and exotic places...you know me all too well! I recently was looking through a *National Geographic Traveler* magazine that I have at home and lo and behold, there was a beautiful picture taken in Armenia of a small monastery surrounded by a lush green hillside with SHEEP grazing nearby. I thought, if this is what Armenia looks like, I'm going to love it. I will definitely be brining my hiking boots! How many suitcases will I be allowed to take??

I love and miss you very much!

Karen xoxo

* * *

FROM: Tim Carlin

TO: Everyone

SENT: February 5, 2003 5:50 PM

Hi Everyone,

Well, it's about time I wrote everyone and brought you up to date on the around-the-world cruise I am taking. First, before I get started, I apologize for any typos or grammatical mistakes, but I feel it's probably more important to get the email out than proofread it for publishing, so sit back and enjoy the journey.

I will try to send you an email once every 5-7 days from the ship. By the way, right now we are cruising the Tasmanian Sea en route to Tasmania. Australia and the Tasmanian devil, among other things. You can send me an email free of charge to QE2@cruisemail.com. Under the subject, put Tim Carlin Room 4241. When you write, I encourage you to ask any questions and I'll comment back to you in my next email.

My fiancé, Karen, will forward the email to you upon receipt from me, so don't delete anything from Karen Gecas, because it contains information about "the voyage of six continents." Yes, that's right, I said fiancé. Karen and I are planning to get married the 6th of May in St. Thomas in a beautiful outdoor ceremony. How we met is a story in and of itself, so I won't go into detail here but rather when I return and see you in person or talk to you over the phone. After a great honeymoon, the plan is for us both to relocate to the country of Armenia, where I will assume the post of Bilateral Affairs Officer to the country of Armenia. Orders are in the works so everything is subject to change, but that's the plan right now. According to Karen, my real job will be to actually travel around Eastern Europe, visiting strange and exotic places. I truly look forward to introducing each and every one of you to her.

My journey started from New York on 5 January. We traveled to Fort Lauderdale where I took a great Everglades tour and came face to face with a ten-foot alligator, among other things. I took a thirty-minute ride on an airboat into the Everglades National Park. Going south, we visited Curacao, which is next to Aruba, then we transited the Panama Canal and its locks. Going through Gatun (sp) Lake was beautiful. After visiting Panama City, it was on to Acapulco. I have great memories of Acapulco, having vacationed there with my family two times. I just want to say to Jeff, my brother, and John, my brother-in-law, the jet skis and parasailing are still alive and well. What a fun city, still very authentic and not Americanized like Cancun. The cliff divers, bay swimming, and the flea market were fun. I ate some homemade burritos, and they were delicious with no aftereffects!

That brings me to about the 15th of January, when we cruised the Pacific Ocean up to Los Angeles. There, I met an Army buddy from Germany, Art Kovach. As always, we had a great time, visiting the *Queen Mary* and the beach boardwalks. The tour of the *Queen Mary* was fascinating. The ship was famous from a time when Ocean Liner cruising was in its heyday. Movie stars and royalty would regularly travel on board. During WWII, it was called the *Grey Ghost* and used as a troop ship. At one point, it transitioned 16,000 troops to the European theater. This adds new meaning to the term "hot bunking." If you are ever in Long Beach, California, I encourage you to see this historical wonder. Next, it was on to Hawaii.

Having been there before, I decided to do the Hawaiian Royalty Walk. Woody Fern, who is a local master storyteller, accompanied us on the tour and wove a great story involving the Kamehameha Statue, the Iolani Palace, and the original home of Queen Liliuokalani. It was a nice tour and something totally different. Having visited Pearl Harbor before, it was interesting seeing the reaction of people who saw it for the first time. I was impressed with the many non-Americans who expressed their condolences to me upon their return to the ship. En route to Hawaii, we encountered rough seas. Thirty to forty foot waves were the norm for two days. It put many of the passengers onboard down and out. We could see from our rooms the waves crashing over the bow as Tchaikovsky's *Four Seasons* was playing because of the closed-circuit connection onboard. Channel three always has the bow and classical music playing twenty-four hours a day. It was fun to watch the wave then feel it in your room.

After Hawaii, it was on to the South Pacific, Tahiti, and the Island of Moorea. They were both beautiful but I give the nod to Moorea. They filmed the mountains from Moorea in the movie "South Pacific" to depict "Bali Hai." It was wonderful, definitely a place Karen and I will go back to. We docked in Captain Cook Bay and I sent Karen some pictures, so if you live in Chicago she will be glad to show them to you since I won't be home until the 18th of April. During my stay in Moorea, I swam with, fed, and touched these 6-foot stingrays. These critters were big, and I have to say after being dropped off in the middle of the ocean I was a little apprehensive. But everything went well, and the water was crystal clear, and yes it was warm!

After visiting French Polynesia (Tahiti and Moorea), it was on to New Zealand. I forgot to mention: when we crossed the equator, there was this big King Neptune ceremony where the *QE2* crew staff rubbed fish oil and salmon all over you then pushed you in the pool. We were called pollywogs and it was a lot of fun. Karen has a picture of the ceremony, along with Moorea, the stingrays, and "Bali Hai." We took three days to get to New Zealand and in the process lost a day by crossing the International Date Line. We each received a certificate for the crossing under our door the following morning.

By the way, every day we receive a ship's program and travel guide for the city we are visiting. In addition, we receive an abstract from the *New York Times* and live satellite feeds of BBC or CNN World if we are in range. A day doesn't go by where there isn't a discussion about Iraq, North Korea, or the Shuttle. Every morning, there is a discussion group led by a priest and a rabbi from 9:30 to 10:15. They kind of get everybody riled up then moderate the discussion. Well, you can imagine the diversity of views. We have 1,600 people onboard from all over the world. What a great learning laboratory. Everyone is eager for my viewpoint because they know I'm in the active National Guard. Recognizing I'm an unofficial ambassador for the US, I make sure I think before I speak. I must be doing OK because people still ask me my opinion on numerous issues. Regardless, everyone is praying onboard the ship that things get worked out. Yes, I am on call and my boss Colonel Vonderschmidt knows how to reach me by phone and email. Colonel V was kind enough to let me complete annual training and drill early in order to take this journey. Sir, I promise I'll be back in time for April drill, if not sooner!

Auckland, New Zealand was great. We saw the Americas' Cup along with beautiful countryside, to include New Zealand's version of Yellowstone National Park and the tallest building in the Southern Hemisphere, the Sky Tower. An interesting cultural note: the youth of New Zealand bungee jump off the Tower, which is similar to the CN tower in Toronto. It seems they're into bungee jumping off anything higher than 5o meters. I was tempted but I didn't do it. Maybe I'll do a tandem with Karen when we return someday.

Well, that pretty much brings me up to date. Currently, we are cruising the Tasmanian Sea en route to Tasmania and the Tasmanian devil. I am going to try and visit Port Arthur, which is an old penal colony. Australia is where the British used to send all their criminals until the turn of the 1900s. I'll send everyone an update in a couple of days. In the meantime, I welcome your questions.

God Bless!

Tim

* * *

LETTER FROM VUNG TAU, VIETNAM

By Lt. Col. Tim Carlin, U.S. Army Reserve

March 11, 2003

I am on the *QE2*, anchoring at Phu My Port, Ba Ria in Vung Tau province. It is 9 AM, and a hot muggy haze hangs over the city. It is 90 degrees and very humid. For the American Vietnam veterans onboard, this is a highly emotional experience. We arrive in this port by tender, a thirty-minute ride. This is the poorest port we have visited.

As we debark the tender, we are welcomed by a man using a bullhorn who speaks in broken English. A cordon of ten young Vietnamese women also welcomes us. They are wearing brightly colored dresses, which are called "so dai," and they say hello to us and clap. Women all over Vietnam wear these attractive dresses.

We board a reasonably decent bus for a three-hour ride to the Cu Chi tunnels. Our tour guide, Nguyen, is about twenty-six years old and is polite and treats us with great respect.

We travel on highway 51 towards Saigon and turn off to Cu Chi. After Nguyen introduced himself, he gave us a history of Vietnam and that country's struggle for freedom from various invaders. Then, earnestly, he sang the Vietnamese national anthem. We appreciated his song and applauded.

The Vietnamese are very patriotic, just as Americans are. The Vietnamese flag, which is red with a gold star in the center, flies everywhere, from homes, businesses, factories, government buildings, and barracks.

Saigon has a population of 8 million. Those 8 million use 25 million motorbikes. A madhouse! Our driver beeps his horn every two seconds for the entire trip. I have my military earplugs, and I put them in.

The road is built of rough concrete and dirt. There are no sidewalks and no grass. Homes and businesses are situated not far from the road. I see Vietnamese women outside. They are covered from head to toe and wear conical hats. Our guide explains that the women like white skin, so they keep covered.

The streets are open, and there are no traffic lights.

We made a rest stop at 11:40. This facility, which is part of a private home, is primitive. I liken it to a pigs' trough with a pan.

Off highway 51, we turned onto highway 1, which is an all-dirt road. We passed the site of the former Australian military base, which was active during the Vietnam War.

We crossed the Saigon River. Many rice paddies here. We also passed the Vietnamese Non-Commissioned Officers' Military Academy, which is a three-year school.

The vegetation reminds me of Honduras, when I was stationed with the 101st Airborne Division during Big Pine exercises.

We passed a huge Viet Cong cemetery that stretched for miles. The vegetation is getting thicker.

We arrived at Cu Chi and had a Vietnamese lunch outside the war memorial to Vietnamese veterans, which is on the Saigon River. The countryside is lush and green. It is pleasant to eat under thatch-roofed huts. I wandered off by myself, found a place that sells books, and bought a fascinating book on the past and present history of the Cu Chi tunnels.

We boarded a bus to the tunnels. These tunnels are 125 miles in length. A few of the tunnels have been widened to accommodate Western tourists; many are too narrow for Westerners. It is very dark and claustrophobic inside. I had to crouch the entire way, and I also proceeded on my hands and knees.

The tunnel led into a meeting room and then on to a supply room. Further on was a surgery center. I tunneled my way out. I have the utmost respect for the United States and South Vietnamese soldiers, called "tunnel rats," who used these tunnels during the Vietnam War. Emerging from the tunnels, one finds the craters caused by B-52 bombs.

Next, we went to a patrol staging area. This reminded me of Ranger school at Fort Benning. Here, there was a framed picture of Ho Chi Minh and an operational map of Vietnam, in which the country was broken into sectors.

We saw a 1965 propaganda film on the heroism of the Cu Chi fighters, which I purchased. It is an authentic film, produced by the North Vietnamese.

After leaving the briefing area, I visited the various displays and had my picture taken with men and women dressed as Viet Cong, who also served as guides.

I purchased some mementos. Very cheap. Two books, the video, twenty postcards, taffy, and a soft drink came to 9 U.S. dollars.

On the way back, I noticed an intricate canal system, which connects the Saigon River to outlying rice paddies. Farmers were loading rice onto sampans for transportation to the city. As we entered the outskirts of Saigon, we passed many small shops selling a wide variety of goods. Washing machines, textiles, jewelry, cookware, food, baby supplies, cock fighting supplies, newspapers, ornate coffins—everything imaginable.

Buildings here are only 3 or 4 stories high, and on the streets there is a veritable sea of humanity.

I went to the world-famous Rex Hotel; there was an open bar on the rooftop. Reportedly, foreign correspondents stayed here during the Vietnam War, and U.S. intelligence also functioned here. From the roof, there is a magnificent view of the city at nightfall.

I should mention that on the way to Saigon, there are no stop signs, stoplights, or dividing lines on the road. The road was so crowded it might have been the New York City marathon on motorbikes.

We proceeded to the New World Saigon Hotel, where we had dinner and entertainment by Vietnamese dancers; later, I visited the night market. The next morning, we went to the historical museum, where there was an informative exhibit on Vietnam's history.

After that, we saw an appealing puppet show.

The Jade Emperor's Pagoda was our next stop. I bought three live birds for a dollar, then made a wish and set them free. This temple was built at the turn of the century, and various deities are displayed there. The air was filled with incense and smoke, but I could see the imposing Emperor through it. Carved wooden panels in the "Hall of Ten Hells" describe the fate of the wicked.

In 1975, the American Consulate here was evacuated. That building was taken down and a new consulate built, and we visited the new one. On the way, there are elegant colonial buildings and the Notre Dame Cathedral.

After that, we visited the old presidential palace, now called Reunification Hall. An extraordinary experience! I saw the President's cabinet room, another meeting room, and underground command and control tunnels. Here, there was an escape tunnel to the Saigon River and the command and control bunker beneath the palace where the South Vietnamese President had direct contact with the Pentagon. We walked in the tunnel where one of the Presidents was assassinated.

The equipment that still remained was United States issue, and that included old radio systems and government desks and chairs. Also, there was Russian tank #390. That's the tank that was driven right up to the presidential palace on the 3oth of April, 1975. I couldn't resist having my picture taken in it.

Next, I had my picture taken in the Chinese-made tank

#893. That tank was the one that crashed the gates of the palace. I was fifteen years old when I saw these events on television. It was an emotional experience for me to see, firsthand, the relics of history that shaped my childhood.

We also visited a lacquer factory and then boarded the bus for our three-hour trip back to port. Once onboard, the Captain told us that not many cruise ships stop at Vietnam. We were one of the few that did, and I was very glad.

I told her of the funny things that were going on, and she'd write me back about wedding planning. That's how we corresponded, emailing back and forth. On the ship, though, the staff would print out the email and slip it under my door. I looked forward to those emails every morning when I woke up. It was exciting to go throughout the world and get these letters, knowing she was getting mine.

My travel diary was for Karen, describing it all to her so it was almost like she was there with me. She loves travel as much as I do.

I was onboard the ship as a gentleman host. Again, that meant dancing with women who either didn't have partners or whose partners didn't want to dance or didn't know how. Dancing with the ladies and making them feel young and vibrant again was a different type of service. It made me feel really good, and I'm sure they enjoyed it too.

I was only forty-two at the time. A lot of the women were older, mostly in their sixties or seventies, and some even in their eighties. It is one of the most wonderful things in the world to look into the blue eyes of an eighty-year-old woman and to give her joy and make her feel eighteen again by dancing with her.

I was able to do that for many of these women.

They had all lived long and interesting lives. Some had been nurses during World War II. Some had recently lost their husbands. All of them had a story.

One particular woman was Jewish and had lived through a Nazi concentration camp as a little girl. She was a big believer in America and what we had done for her and the French in World War II. On certain nights, I would wear my uniform when I danced with her, and we talked about my time at West Point and in the Army. It really made me feel wonderful to bring that alive for her, to make her feel young and wonderful again in the absence of her husband who had passed.

Another was a Polish woman who had two rooms: one room to live in, and another room for all her beautiful gowns. Every night, she would have on a different, beautiful gown. This wasn't like the Carnival Cruise. This was a high-end cruise. The men wore tuxedoes and the ladies wore evening gowns every night. If you think of how they dressed every night on the Titanic, that's how we dressed.

I was honored to be able to treat these women with empathy, dignity, and respect, to look at them as the women they were and are, and to bring back that past for them.

Another woman I danced with, Ann Post, was a famous sculptress from New York. Her husband had died twenty years prior to the cruise. She was a diminutive lady, maybe five feet tall and very slender, very well spoken. She lived in Washington Square, in New York City, right by NYU.

Every morning, we would meet to talk about politics and play Scrabble. She was an excellent Scrabble player. I remember getting beat 150 to ten. If I had a good day, it might be 150 to twenty-five. She would always tease me and say, "I just want you to know that I'm very impressed with what your English professors at West Point taught you."

She knows West Point has very good education, but she couldn't help but to tease me.

We'd always have what she called peasant toast in the morning: thicker, seven-grain toast I introduced her to. We talked about politics—she was a little more left, I was a little more right—and we had fun talking and teasing, agreeing on some things and agreeing to disagree on others.

Every night, between seven thirty and eight o'clock, she would watch me dancing. I would walk up to her, bow, and ask, "Would you like to dance?"

"No," she always said. "My husband passed away twenty years ago. I don't think it would be appropriate, but I do enjoy watching you and seeing the dancing."

Finally, one night midway through the trip, she said, "Yes, I'll do one dance."

We did a nice, slow foxtrot and talked as we went around the dance floor. At the end of the music, she had a big smile on her face.

"I thoroughly enjoyed this," she said. "Good night."

And she slowly walked off very definitively, with purpose.

The next night, we did the same thing. In fact, every night thereafter we would have one dance together before she would retire to bed.

We became such good friends that when I started my financial advisory business, she was one of my first clients. She invited me and Karen to New York City. As our wedding gift, she gave us a beautiful African teak wood sculpture of a man and woman embracing, one that she had shown in the Metropolitan Museum of Art for many years. We really appreciate it—it's absolutely one of our most beautiful and cherished pieces.

Embrace by Ann Post.

When we were in her home, she asked, "Tell me what piece you want for your wedding, to represent your marriage. I want to do this for you."

We picked that one because it spoke to us. She said, "Yes, that's my very first romantic sculpture that I did when I was eighteen years old."

I like the concept of romance and deep connection.

I danced every night for three-and-a-half months, and I corresponded with Karen every day.

"I DO"

As the ship got closer and closer to coming back home, I was filled with excitement. I was really looking forward to getting married and settling down with Karen, and I was extremely thrilled to be coming back.

She pulled up in a limousine to pick me up at the airport. I had my baggage in hand, and after such a long trip, it felt really good to be home and see Karen.

I gave Karen the most beautiful ring, one I'd found in South Africa. She loved it.

Ours was almost like an arranged marriage because we hadn't really dated for long—but we'd stayed true to one another. Some people may have wondered whether she'd still be there when I got back. After all, we'd only known each other for two weeks before the cruise. Although there may have been temptations on the ship or back in Chicago, that didn't change our plan to get married. We were beginning to set the underpinnings of a good foundation for our relationship: we had good communication, and we did whatever we said we were going to do.

Two weeks after my arrival home, on May 6, 2003, Karen and I were married in St. Thomas, US Virgin Islands.

You may now kiss the bride.

We had a destination wedding with nineteen people in attendance. My mom and dad were there, as was Karen's mom. Her sister was her maid of honor, and my longtime military buddy was my best man. Both of us had some friends there. Some of my friends from the ship came. We did a beautiful Catamaran sunset cruise the night before, followed by dinner on the beach with a calypso band playing.

The day of, we were wed at the Marriott Frenchman's Reef, at two o'clock in the afternoon, overlooking the beautiful ocean. It was a bright and sunny day and the wind kept it cool. We got married between two palm trees with the ocean behind us and our guests taking in the view. There was a little gazebo to the right where we had cake and champagne afterward.

The happy couple in the gazebo.

Karen had a very classy gown that embodied her graceful and flowing spirit.

Everything was just gorgeous. The event was a beautiful, small wedding in picturesque St. Thomas. Karen had exactly the wedding she wanted—an exotic outdoor destination wedding.

Stan and Lita, friends from my trip around the world.

After the ceremony, Karen and I performed a beautiful waltz. Everybody gathered around to watch—this was before *Dancing with the Stars* got big, so it wasn't something people often saw. We could both dance pretty well, and people enjoyed it very much. It was kind of like a story in dance of how we met, our courtship, and how we fell in love.

The next day, we took a ferry to St. John with our best man, Richard, and his wife, Debbie. They are wonderful people, and we are still friends and see each other to this day, most recently watching the Kansas City Chiefs' victory in Super Bowl LIV.

Karen and I hiked and explored St. John. Anytime we heard music playing—in the hotel, someone playing the piano, or salsa music on the street—we would stop and dance together. People would stop and watch us, then clap when we finished as we kissed.

We also got to know each other better—it was the first time we were all alone for more than just a few hours. We briefly had a feeling of, "Okay, everyone's gone. The excitement of the wedding is over. Now what do we do?"

CLIMBING EVER HIGHER

As our ten-year anniversary present to each other, Karen and I climbed Mount Kilimanjaro.

Before I met her, she had climbed the Himalayan Mountains. She wanted to do a safari trip, and I said, "Hey, as long as we're going that far, let's kill two birds with one stone and do a safari *and* climb Mount Kilimanjaro!"

Karen thought about it quietly. All of a sudden she said, "Why not!"

We had to prepare for almost a year, both to train for the hike and, perhaps even more importantly, to get all the clothing and proper gear we would both need on our adventure.

We took three weeks off in December to do both the safari and the climb. We flew into Arusha, Tanzania, and signed up with a travel firm called Wilderness Travel, which is a wonderful firm that does exotic hiking destinations all over the world. They took us across the flat African prairie to the base of a huge mountain, fifty miles in diameter and 19,500 feet high—Mount Kilimanjaro.

At the base of the mountain, we saw elephants, lions, Cape buffalo, leopards, monkeys, and giraffes.

As we started climbing, we had thirty Sherpas with us, carrying food and oxygen. They also carried a mess tent and supplies—anything we may need down (or should I say up!) the road. Because we were climbing over the Christmas holiday, there were only four hikers on this trip—me and Karen, a mom celebrating her fiftieth birthday, and her son. We also had a ranger with us, who had a weapon in case we got charged by a Cape buffalo or other wild game.

Pre-climb Masai warrior ceremony.

We started at about fifteen hundred feet above sea level. It was dense jungle and very hot because Mount Kilimanjaro is at the equator; we were quickly drenched in sweat. Then, as we went up, it got colder and colder—we went through seven temperate climate zones as we climbed. In the lower zones, we saw birds and monkeys. In the upper zone, we saw the glacier. Who would think that in the middle of Africa, you can have two-hundred-foot glaciers and three to five feet of snow on the ground?

We had to pack and prepare for all the different temperatures too. We started with very light layers and then kept adding clothing. We slept in two-person pup tents, and we had to work together as a team, especially when we got up into the higher, colder elevations. Karen and I also had to be comfortable living together in very tight quarters.

Me, Karen, and the pup tent at base camp.

One night when we had climbed to about 17,500 feet, the temperature outside was about ten degrees and the wind howled around us—and we realized we had to go to the restroom.

We quickly learned to keep an empty water jug nearby. If we had to go in the middle of the night, we'd wake up and help each other: one person would hold the light and the other would hold the jug, to make sure we didn't have to go outside the tent. Karen had a device that allowed her to eliminate waste like a man, without having to sit. The tent was small and tight, it was freezing cold—and the experience was another great way to strengthen our bond. Under those difficult conditions, we had to communicate and depend on one another, skills I had been perfecting since Canisius, West Point, and Ranger School.

UP AND DOWN

We summited on Christmas morning, a beautiful, clear day. The mountain is somewhat flat at the very top because it used to be a volcano, so we were able to walk across it and look down into the valley through the clouds below us.

On top of Mount Kilimanjaro.

After that, we started back down. We descended ten thousand feet the first day and nine thousand the second. It took seven days to climb up—but only two days to come back down. The travel firms want hikers off the mountain quickly because there's less oxygen higher up, so you can get mountain sickness, which can be deadly. It's not like Everest, but we saw crosses along the route, marking people who had passed away.

After hiking three days, halfway there!

At about ten to twelve thousand feet, we saw the bones of an elephant. We asked the Sherpa what had happened, and he said that the elephant had most likely been looking for water and got confused so it went up the mountain instead of down. There's less and less water as you go up, so it becomes more and more barren.

The mountain itself was well taken care of and very clean. It wasn't like Mount Everest where everything is littered and overcrowded. We packed everything up, didn't leave anything behind, and were very aware of the conservation efforts.

While we were going up, I learned the alphabet in Swahili

from the guides. I'm always trying to learn new things, so my guides first taught me the word for "A like apple," and then I would learn "apple" in Swahili too. Then I learned "B for boy." As we hiked, they would call out the letter of the alphabet and I would say the Swahili word. Before we got to the top, I knew the whole alphabet and corresponding words in Swahili.

English was their second language, so I would also tell them American jokes and they would laugh. We spent some time building a relationship with each other, to where they understood America better and we learned more about their country. It was an amazing experience.

Back at base camp after descending Mount Kilimanjaro.

Then we did the safari. On the drive over to the Ngoron-goro Crater in Tanzania, we saw all these animals roaming around: lions in one place, elephants in the other. We saw hyenas, cheetahs, and other species I didn't even know the names for. It was like a zoo with no gates. And they all got along—until one of them got hungry.

We had traveled to the Vatican in 2010 and Israel in 2011, but Africa connected everything together—we were like Adam and Eve in the Garden of Eden with animals freely roaming around. Africa really connected the dots on believing in a higher being, showing the evolution of the way some people worship and understanding how we're so insignificant individually, yet at the same time, significant as part of a higher power's plan.

It felt like I could trace my ancestry back forty thousand years, back to Africa in the area that is now Ethiopia. It wouldn't surprise me if a lot of us originally started from that Garden of Eden.

It was, no question, our best trip ever.

WHEN IT'S RIGHT, IT'S RIGHT

I'm proud to say that Karen and I have been happily married since 2003.

Fundraising event for the West Point Parents Club.

Some people would say that it was crazy to propose to her after only three days of our meeting—that I should have been more cautious and judicious. Agreeing so quickly to marry was, in fact, out of character for both of us—but acting on my gut instincts and not heeding the advice of others has worked out nicely.

Even though we'd only been together in person for three-and-a-half weeks prior to getting married, I knew it was right—and when you know it's right, you don't want to let that opportunity go by. Sometimes you have to listen to your gut, not what other people may say, and take action based on your experiences and what you believe to be true. It may not always work out—but sometimes it does.

When I asked Karen to marry me, after sharing all the things I'd done—going to West Point, being in the military, working with PepsiCo and Phillips, learning how to dance, living in Chicago, going overseas in different situations—she looked at me, processing it all in her head, and she agreed, because she knew in her gut that it was right, as I did.

Karen appreciated the experiences I brought to our marriage. From her, I needed stability, loyalty, someone who was going to be rock solid. We complement each other to this day. We try new and different things that push our boundaries and make us uncomfortable because we continue coming up with new ideas to grow and develop.

It's still not boring!

CHAPTER 5

Think Long-Term

When I was a little boy, eleven or twelve years old, I had a newspaper route.

When the newspaper truck came each evening, I wheeled my blue *Buffalo Evening News* wagon down the block to pick up my stack of 110 papers to be delivered—every day except Sunday. Most of the other delivery boys were older than I was, and I thought it was great to be with them. As each of us loaded up our wagon, Sammy Speciale's mom checked our names on a list, and off we'd go.

My route was pretty easy; it comprised six apartment buildings, each three stories tall with eight apartments on each floor. I balanced twenty-four papers on my head, using one hand to hold them in place and the other to throw the papers to the doorsteps where they needed to be. I made a big circle to deliver the papers. I had memorized who got a paper, so I didn't even have to check my list—I'd just grab a newspaper off my head and drop it at the door. I hustled back to my wagon for more papers and started another round.

Once a week, I collected money from the customers. I kept a card for each customer on a ring and, when they paid their weekly amount, I used a hole puncher to mark their card and mine. It taught me very early on about how to be a businessman.

Many of my customers were older. They often asked me in to talk and spend time with them. One elderly woman taught me how to make fudge. I enjoyed our comfortable conversations and learning what they taught me.

In the cold snow of winter and heat of summer, through the flowers of the spring and falling leaves of autumn, I consistently and faithfully pulled my wagon and delivered the papers.

The route was much harder in freezing temperatures when the wind whipped snow and ice to sting my face. If Dad was home, he often pulled the wagon for me in bad weather.

My dad also taught me about mutual funds. Every month,

he would help me take twenty-five dollars from running my own little business and invest it into mutual funds. I learned early about the effect of compounding interest.

Once I started wrestling in high school, my brother, Jeff, took over the route. We each held it for four years—eight years of delivering papers in one family.

I saved every last bit of money I earned. By the time I went to college, I had enough for a down payment on my first car—a Pontiac Firebird, black with a maroon interior. It was like the KITT car that David Hasselhoff would ride in *Knight Rider.*

LOOK TO THE FUTURE

I learned early in my life that if I wanted something, I didn't have to go into debt to pay for it. I looked to the future, thinking long term, rather than, "Oh, I have a nickel in my pocket, I'm going to go spend it."

Putting away a little bit of money is a big deal because, down the road, it can put you in a good financial position. Money gives you the power to choose, not just what you buy, but also how you live. The power of choice is freedom—but you only get that by choosing wisely.

When I was growing up, it was the bomb to have Converse sneakers, the ones with the star on the side and, even more importantly, stars on the bottom of the sole that would wear away as you used the sneakers. Converse All-Stars were *the* sneakers to have—but they were expensive.

I asked my mom, "Can I please have a pair of Converse sneakers?"

"No," she said, "We can't afford Converse sneakers. We'll get you a pair from Kmart."

I couldn't get what I wanted all the time, but that taught me to sacrifice and to delay gratification. I realized that one of the reasons I began saving and ultimately got into financial services was because I never wanted to be in the position again where I couldn't get Converse sneakers if I wanted them.

I knew that nothing was going to be handed to me, so I'd have to work for whatever I was going to get.

You always have to look to the future and think about who you want to be—and what you want to have. What's most important to *you?*

As a little boy, it was very important for me to have protection and my security needs met. As a young man, I started thinking about what I wanted to do and what I wanted to have in order to feel secure, protected, and satisfied.

I didn't grow up at the same socioeconomic level where I am now, and that's good. It's important to never forget where you came from, so you're appreciative of what you have. I know that what I have now is certainly a lot better than what I had growing up.

My middle-class, blue-collar roots are still very much a part of me. I know that life can get pretty miserable if you don't have options. In the back of my mind, I always have the fear of not having enough money, of losing the option to create my own destiny.

Everything I do in life is calculated to where I'm looking further out to see what the implications are if I do it or don't do it. I'm always trying to figure out and project in the future: *if I do this, that will happen.* What are the ramifications of a course of action based on the facts and assumptions I know now?

I've always had strategic intent, not for selfish reasons but to understand how the decisions I make now will impact my future.

GROWING UP EARLY

My dad was a police officer and my mom was a home-maker. We certainly didn't have an extravagant lifestyle. But my parents loved us—my brother, sister, and me—and provided for us in our modest duplex.

During the time I grew up, Buffalo was a hard-luck city because the steel mills were closing. It was the Rust Belt. You really had to be a scrapper in more ways than one.

My parents taught me great values, but when they met, they hadn't finished college; they were only high school graduates. My dad went back to college once he was on the police force, when he was in his thirties. My mom didn't finish college until I was out of high school and at West Point.

When I was a young boy, before I was a teenager, my dad wasn't around much because of work either as a state trooper or police officer working odd shifts. When your dad's gone for a week or two as a state trooper, that feels like two years to a young kid. My mom was essentially a single parent during that time, and she needed help, so I couldn't be as much of a kid—I had to help with my younger siblings. I was the man of the house, so I had to grow up quickly. I had to be more responsible. My mom would always remind me, "You're the oldest, so you have to help me take care of the kids."

I took care of my younger brother, Jeff, who is four-and-a-half years younger than me, and my sister, Roxane, who is a year younger than Jeff. When you're little, that's a world of difference. When he was five, I was ten—and I could do a lot more to help than he could. My sister was four, and my mom was outnumbered. There were three of us and only one of her, so she turned me into a mini-adult.

I served at an early age. My mom was young herself. When I was nine, she was only twenty-six. At times, she was overwhelmed, just like any young mom with three children would be. So even though I was a little guy, I got serious and helped get my siblings dressed for school, held their hands as we crossed the street, made sure they got to school, and protected them.

It snowed every single day in the winter—and we had a big driveway. Not only did I have to shovel the driveway when I got home from delivering papers, but I had to shovel the concrete patio area in the backyard as well. Sometimes, as a little kid, I would start at ten in the morning and not finish until two or three in the afternoon—but I would scrape all the snow, all the way down to the concrete. When it snowed and then froze, it would be really hard, but I would still do the whole thing. I was so proud of myself, a little worker bee.

I also had my siblings help me and my mom clean the house. I was kind of like a little manager.

I was a man ahead of my time—a little, intense man. I never really had this fun, carefree, lackadaisical childhood. I was always organizing something or making sure my brother and sister were okay. And that was a good thing. It taught me independence, drive, and discipline. I had a good childhood. I didn't have a *typical* childhood, but who really does?

MY LIFE PATH

At each stage in my life, I looked to the future before making the decision that would best set me up for success.

Canisius was a college preparatory school, so I knew that doing well there, getting involved, and being a good student would set me up well to go to a great college. And it did—it allowed me to get into West Point.

I knew that going to West Point would set me up for a great career in the military, which would then set me up for another great career in the business world. Serving in the military is always good to have on your resume.

Thinking long-term, I knew that if I got qualified from Ranger School, Airborne School, and Air Assault School, I would be able to join good-quality units like the 101st Airborne and 2nd Armored Cavalry Regiment, both of which were rapid response or forward deployed and more likely to be engaged in combat if that situation came up. I knew that would be very good both for furthering my career and in my experiences serving others.

Once I made the decision to leave the military, I knew that joining a top-rated Fortune 5oo company would give me the experience and knowledge of how to operate in corporate America. Instead of going to a smaller company initially, which I knew I could always do later, I chose PepsiCo. That taught me a lot about business—so much so that, as I've mentioned, I was recruited to Phillips 66, another Fortune 5oo company.

A year after I retired from active duty in the Army, I joined the Kansas Army National Guard. Deciding to do so meant some sacrifice—weekend duty and a couple weeks of summer training every year. I served for another fifteen years, and by doing so, it gave me a pension and complete medical care. I had to focus on that service alongside building my life in the private sector. In 2006, I retired with the rank of full colonel.

This series of building blocks led me to my forties when, with all this experience, I realized I was ready to start my own business with Edward Jones. That allowed me to take everything I'd learned up to that point—and everything I continue learning—to other people, helping them look to their own futures as well.

I'll tell you the rest of that story in the next chapter.

EL FUTURO

At Canisius, we were given a choice of electives, and I wanted to learn a second language. I chose Spanish because I knew it would be very helpful for me throughout my life. Even in the late 1970s, I realized that, living in the United States, it would be appropriate and useful to know more about Hispanic culture.

I continued studying Spanish at West Point for two years.

In the Army, my first duty assignment was with the 2nd Battalion, 320th Field Artillery Regiment of the 101st Airborne Division at Fort Campbell, Kentucky. Three months later, I was deployed to a hot zone in Central America.

I volunteered to interview to fill the position of platoon leader with a different unit that actually got deployed, the 3rd Battalion, 319th Field Artillery. It was 1983, and this was one of the first deployments into a hot zone since the Vietnam War, so there was a lot riding on this; they wanted to make sure they filled the position with the best of the best.

When I went in for my interview, the first thing the commander liked was that I was a West Pointer—he was too.

Next, he liked that I was Ranger qualified; that spoke volumes. I had known that getting the Ranger tab would open up opportunities for me, allowing me to better serve others in the military. But perhaps the most important thing was that when he greeted me in Spanish, I responded in Spanish too.

"Do you know Spanish well?" he asked.

"I know enough to be dangerous—and to get around."

That opened the door the rest of the way, and he selected me on the spot.

THE MISSION

We then deployed and were charged with setting up a base camp just outside of Trujillo, Honduras, a coastal city in the north with about thirty thousand residents. At the time, we were in the middle of an undeclared conflict.

Me and my Honduran counterpart.

One day, I was given a mission to go with one of my soldiers, my driver, to meet with a CIA agent who was working undercover at Litton Industries. Founded in 1934, Litton Industries was purchased in 1956 by Charles Bates Thornton, a Pentagon official who transformed it from a radio-engineering firm into a major producer of military components and ships. It was perfect cover for a CIA agent who was trying to get arms and other supplies into and around El Salvador, Nicaragua, and Honduras.

We had to drive about one hundred miles along rutted roads and twisty mountainsides through vegetation to the capital city of Tegucigalpa. I was directed to park our military vehicle—back then, we had Jeeps, not Humvees—away from where we were meeting and to wear civilian clothes to avoid drawing attention to ourselves. I was also directed to bring a loaded pistol in case I needed it.

We arrived in Tegucigalpa and parked our Jeep far away from the hotel. After hotel registration, the question was, should I carry my loaded weapon with me or should I leave it in the hotel room? I can't reveal the exact details of our mission, but there was danger involved. We were in Honduras, so we were relatively safe there, but factions were trying to disrupt the government and possibly join with Ortega in Nicaragua.

I had to evaluate the risk of walking through the streets with my pistol versus trying to make our way without one. There were demonstrations going on throughout the city, both for and against the government, a clash between capitalism and communism.

For better or for worse, I chose the latter. I reasoned the chance of having to use my pistol was more probable en route to Tegulcigulpa through the jungle where we were alone and could face possible ambushes rather than in the concrete jungle of the city with the Honduran forces all around us. We put our guns between the mattresses in our hotel room and left to do our business. We had purchased some clothes in Trujillo that matched what everybody else was wearing, so, dressed in non-American clothing and with my darker skin and hair, I was able to fly under the radar.

Fortunately, we didn't get into any trouble. We met with the CIA agent and had a conference with him and a couple of other folks on logistics and supplies. The objective was to do a deal, pay the deal off to get the necessary supplies and equipment we needed to carry on our mission, and make sure we were able to bring them to the Contras who were fighting Ortega and the Sandinistas.

I was scared because I was thinking, "If somebody goes in the hotel room and takes our weapons, we're really in trouble."

The gamble had paid off, however—when we returned to the hotel, the pistols were still where we had left them.

While in Honduras, I was promoted to first lieutenant, so when I got back after a nine-month deployment, I was no longer the low man on the totem pole. I was reassigned back to my unit upon returning from the mission. My time with 101st Airborne was a very good time. I was very proud about my service in such a historic unit.

This is the unit featured in the film *Saving Private Ryan*—

Matt Damon's character was in the 101st Airborne—and in *The Deer Hunter* with Robert DeNiro. This unit was also one of two that did a parachute drop behind the lines at Normandy on D-Day (the other being the 82nd Airborne). And in the Battle of the Bulge, the 101st held the crossroads until Patton's army could rescue them in the snow. The Screaming Eagles—so called because their patch is a bald eagle, the national bird of the United States, screaming, with the word "Airborne" over it—have a long, proud history of serving our country.

I was only twenty-three, but my military training, Ranger training, and being cool under pressure taught me how to size things up and make smart decisions on the fly.

Although that was another example of thinking long-term and looking to the future, it wouldn't be the last.

THE PROPER CARE AND FEEDING OF HUSBANDS...AND WIVES

I like to read books to understand what may happen in the future and learn how to protect my family.

For example, recently I was looking to the future and I realized that Karen and I were in a good place but we weren't communicating the way we had when we first got married. So I picked up a book called *The Proper Care and Feeding of Husbands* by Doctor Laura Schlessinger, and I read that book from cover to cover, highlighting it and taking notes.

Last night, I gave that book to Karen and said, "I'm reading this book because I want to continue to look to the future in our relationship and think long-term about how we can build on what we've done so far. This isn't any criticism of you. I love you. But I highlighted and took notes on what speaks to me and what can help me be a better husband to you. I want you to read this book so we can communicate about it together. That would really mean a lot to me."

I did so because I want my wife to look to the future with me. I want to have an even better relationship going forward, to continue to grow. I don't want to let our marriage sink into mediocrity. And I discovered little things I can do for her that will create a virtuous circle so we can continue to grow and love each other and build going forward. For example, I bring colorful flowers home randomly, and I write goofy love notes on SkinnyPop popcorn (her favorite), which I place around the house where Karen will see them.

Reading the book helped me see new ways to keep things fresh and exciting. Taking notes and sharing them with her was almost like writing a love letter. I tried to show my effort, that I care enough about her and about us to find a sensitive way to improve our communication.

Reading that book helped me realize where my needs might not be getting met—and where her needs may not be met too. I didn't get frustrated with the communication in my marriage; instead, I discovered something new to do what's best for both of us.

We're both in our fifties, and I hope we have twenty or thirty years or even more together. Karen's parents have passed away and my mom recently passed. We have no children, so it's important that we stay strong together, that we don't get isolated, and that we maintain our special bond. Together, we always want to continue to grow and have a wonderful relationship.

WHAT DO YOU WANT TO BE WHEN YOU CONTINUE GROWING UP?

We talk a lot about thinking long-term and looking to the future. When you're a kid, you're asked, "What do you want to be when you grow up?" When you go to college, it's, "What are you majoring in?" Once you start down a career path, however, people stop asking, "What are you going to do?" or "What does your future look like?"

It's just as important after you've already established those things to still be looking to the future. You've got a long future ahead of you, and if you stop thinking about it in your twenties or thirties, you'll miss out on opportunities to grow and evolve.

Sometimes I'll tell my clients to look to the future, and they'll say, "But I'm old."

I say, "No, you're not—you're only sixty. Let's say you live twenty more years. Look back twenty years from today, to when you were forty. Think of all the things that occurred in those twenty years, how much you learned. You still have that time; you can use it to continue learning and having new experiences."

You just have to extend your timeframe. Whenever you make a decision, don't just look at the immediate results; think through the implications of that decision in the long term. Then you can make the best decisions for yourself and the people around you.

Putting away twenty-five dollars a month when I was a little paper boy allowed me to take time off to travel the world, which led me to meet some very fascinating people who became lifelong friends. I could not have known as a young kid that I would get to see the world, but by thinking long-term, you often get to learn something unexpected. It makes you a better person and provides more security, which you can give back to others.

Even deciding to write this book was a long-term decision. It's my legacy, a way to tell my personal story, share memories, and put them on paper. It's a way for clients to get to know me better. All these stories you're reading are ones I've thought through to relate to you, my friends, family members, and clients.

CHANGE IS GOOD—AND INEVITABLE

It's easy to get caught up in nostalgia, feeling sad about how things have changed. I know that's happened to me—when I visited my school, where we used to play, and saw that it's different, I missed those days. But we also have to realize that everything has to change and evolve in order to survive and grow. In the world of finance and capital markets, it is called creative destruction. Companies go out of business and new ones emerge.

Recognizing that pattern gives me comfort. When I go back home to Buffalo and see how things have changed, I see that maybe it's not exactly how I grew up, but I recognize that those memories are a part of me and it's okay for things to change—and that I can grow and change along with them.

Right now, our country is going through a change. It's not necessarily good or bad, but it's something we all need to consider in order to understand where we're going.

Number one, demographically, we have a shift of wealth and power from the baby boomers to the Gen Xers and millennials. That's the first shift. The second shift is a general shift in the country from the center to just left of center. It's not extreme, but the Gen Xers and millennials who are now the largest bloc of voters care more about social issues, green issues, and proper governance. There's also now a shift to have a lot of experiences instead of a lot of things.

There's nothing wrong with these shifts; I just think it's important to educate ourselves about what's happening, where we're going, and why.

When you do, you see that the country is always in transition—and that's okay. It's healthy. It's like cleaning out a closet full of clothes that don't fit anymore, or are worn out, or are out of style. Now we have to make room for new clothes. There may be mourning because emotionally you're getting rid of stuff that you're really attached to, but it's just not part of the fabric of your being or the fabric of our society anymore.

Globalization reached its peak during the 1990s when there was peace all over. The Soviet Union fell, and the Berlin Wall came down. Europe became more integrated. The US didn't have the same amount of terrorism or extremism to contend with. It was a wonderful time, and people traveled and traded freely. There were more McDonald's in China.

Then the attacks of September 11th happened, and that gave rise to a completely different era. Now we have a decrease in globalization—all over the world. Germany doesn't want as many immigrants. Italy doesn't want as many immigrants. The United States doesn't want as many immigrants. We have a global trade war with China over technology and dominance and who's going to be the next superpower. It's a transition. We'll work through it and everything will be fine. The United States ultimately is an idea, and our culture is a gravitational pull for many people all over the world.

But it's important to understand and digest what's happening around us, to evaluate where the world is going, so we can be active good citizens moving forward.

It's also important that if something about who we are is no longer working for us, we have the freedom and flexibility to reinvent ourselves.

CHAPTER 6

Reinvent Yourself

While I was writing this book, I was involved in a car accident. I'm okay, but I had to be hospitalized for a night with a concussion and a fractured nose. I had to get three staples in the back of my head.

I was driving with another couple—Bill was sitting in the front seat with me, and Karen was sitting behind me, in the back seat with Bill's wife, Linda. A car ran a red light and was hit by another car, which then veered off and hit our car head on. The impact was at about forty miles per hour, and we all had to go to the hospital. Linda fractured her sternum, Karen had whiplash, and she and Bill both had contusions on their sternums from the seatbelt— fortunately, everybody was buckled up. The airbags and seatbelts protected us, but the car was totaled. I blacked out and lost some blood, so I had to be kept overnight.

Between my mom passing away and getting in that crash, I had a crazy month.

Fortunately, I have a lifetime of resilience to draw on, so I was able to keep things steady and move on. I realize that's a part of life. For me, it's good therapy to keep everything rolling normally.

It was just a chain reaction of things happening—and it was totally out of my control. I help people, but there was nothing I could do to control that situation. That's why I talk to my clients and try to help them think through as many possible situations as we can. I ask them, "Have you thought about long-term care? Have you thought about disability? What about insurance—do you have an umbrella policy?"

We can only think about what we can control—and it's harder to think about those things we can't control, so we can just try to be as prepared as possible.

MAKING LEMONADE

Even in difficult situations—which I'm going to share more of in this chapter—I learned you can look for the lesson and evaluate how you can improve. You can use that situation to grow even stronger.

You can reinvent yourself.

When I went from being bullied to learning judo, that was a reinvention. Going from trying to be a high school football player to being a high school wrestler was another reinvention. Moving from a full-time active Army career to a civilian career at PepsiCo was a reinvention, as was changing my career from PepsiCo operations to Edward Jones sales. And most recently, I reinvented myself from the more franchise-like firm of Edward Jones to the completely independent firm of V Wealth Advisors.

We're all either growing or shrinking, and upsetting the apple cart a little bit can lead to serious growth. Reinventing yourself helps you stay relevant and have a voice in this world. Reinvention is your will. Do you have a will to survive? If you continue to reinvent yourself and change the environment and the situation around you, then you're going to survive. Reinvention is the pathway to positive thinking, healthy living, and making a difference in people's lives.

By reading, growing, and learning, and by reinventing myself and my business, I can discover new solutions for my clients. Reinvention and learning contribute directly to how I advise people to invest based on a changing economy and the personal situations in my clients' lives.

You're definitely going to be given lemons in life. The trick is how to make lemonade with Stevia out of it. You don't want to put sugar in it, because sugar is the old way. Stevia is a reinvention. It's new and better for you. Life is short, so enjoy the lemonade—but make sure you make it differently than how your grandma made it for you.

JUDO

I got picked on in sixth grade because I was the new kid, after transferring from public school to a private school. I had three things going against me: I looked different, I was smaller than everybody else, and I dressed nicely.

In public school, there was a lot of diversity, but in private school, almost everybody was of Polish descent. With my Italian background, I had darker hair and skin, and I might as well have been from Mars compared to the kids at this school.

We didn't have a lot of money—my parents lived frugally and had saved up to prioritize our education—but my parents always wanted us to look presentable. The kids at Assumption School had been wearing the same uniforms for years, and I showed up with a new jacket and tie. The other kids would wait in the coatroom in the dark until I came to hang up my coat and then they would rough me up a bit.

Instead of getting upset or depressed, I went to my dad

and said, "I need to learn how to defend myself. Can you teach me how to box?"

He didn't know how to box, but Dad had a friend on the police force who knew someone who taught a judo class. He enrolled me in that class at the Ken-Ton YMCA with Sensei Bob every Tuesday and Thursday at 6:30 p.m., and I took all my frustration from what I was facing at school and funneled it into my judo.

Judo is comprised of three basic features: throws, holds, and submissions, which include chokes and arm bars. My specialty became the throw, although I was good at holding my opponent down too. (That would help me later with my wrestling!)

Finishing first at the Eastern Collegiate Judo Association Championship, 1981.

We worked out in the studio at the Y and had competitions in a big gymnasium, all of us in bare feet and wearing a gi, a uniform of loose white pants and a white tunic tied with the different color belts we had earned. The first-level belt is white, and then they progressively get darker up to black belt. Every time I went up a level, we bought a box of fabric dye and changed the color of my belt.

To win a competition, we would earn points for throwing, holding someone down, choking, or arm bars. My first big win came when I was a yellow belt, only my second competition. I stood in the gymnasium for the tournament in front of a couple hundred spectators—but not my mom or dad. They had attended my first competition but couldn't come to this one. I won third place and was so excited to show my dad my trophy when he came to pick me up.

It felt wonderful to win, and that set me on fire.

Soon I was qualifying locally and regularly traveling to out-of-town tournaments with Sensei Bob. We competed all over New York State—Rochester, Brockport, Ithaca—arriving the night before, staying overnight in a hotel, and competing the next morning.

On one of these trips, Sensei Bob drove me and an adult student in his big, red Cadillac. We were on our way home, blasting the radio, and I felt very special.

Over the sound of the radio, we heard a siren. A red light flashed from behind us, shining like blood over the all-white interior of the car. When Sensei Bob pulled over, a state trooper tapped on his window with a flashlight. He shined the light on Sensei Bob, then on the man in the passenger seat. Both men in front were black. Then he directed the beam toward me, the small, white kid sitting in the back seat.

"Whose kid is this?" the state trooper asked.

"We're just coming home from a judo tournament," Sensei Bob explained. "He's one of our competitors."

This was thrilling. Not only had I done well at the tournament; now we were being questioned by a state trooper. How cool was this!

"I'm a police officer," said the older student in front, showing his badge. "The kid's dad is too. We are all friends."

Office McCabe and Sensei Bob made me feel safe and secure. The state trooper bid us safe travels, and it was wonderful to see the trust and respect fellow law enforcement had for each other.

I continued competing, the collection of trophies on top of my dresser grew, and so did my focus and dedication. I loved competing and became one of the studio's star competitors. I threw myself into it and eventually worked my way up to a black belt.

That gave me a tremendous amount of self-confidence because I did really well in the tournaments. It gave me self-confidence with my classmates who were picking on me, but it also gave me a skill that I could later parlay into becoming a better wrestler in high school, where I won a state championship. I then parlayed that into being recruited by West Point for wrestling.

I reinvented myself from a kid who didn't know how to defend himself into someone who couldn't be beat—I asked for help and focused my energy into an outlet that actually helped me achieve other things down the road.

That ability to give my all to something—and not stop until I won—would serve me well later in life too.

STARTING OVER

I got laid off in 2002. I took a year off to figure out what I wanted to do and become. Up until then, I had either been in the Army or in corporate America (you can count the Army as another corporation).

I decided to start over in a new industry, reinventing myself completely.

In late April or early May, before my own wedding, my fiancée and I went down to Oklahoma City for the wedding of the daughter of John Hammann, my best buddy from the military. While there, I saw an advertisement in the daily *Oklahoman* paper: "Be your own business owner! Start your own branch of Edward Jones."

The job was in investments, and I had been investing since I was a little boy.

I love money. It's never been my god, but I learned to understand it from a very young age, as you read in the previous chapter. I knew that if you treat it with respect, you can grow it. I've always been a good steward of my own wealth, and that's why the idea of becoming a financial investor was so appealing to me: I could help other people and earn good money doing it.

I've always wanted to make more than a decent living. In the military, I'd been paid well but I wasn't making the kind of money I could as a small business owner or executive. I wasn't going to be poor on that kind of salary—but I'd never be rich either.

I called up and asked for more information. They told me that it was a franchise and I didn't have to put in any money, but that there was a lot of sweat equity to start. "All you have to do is execute what we tell you to do."

Being a military guy, I thought to myself, "I can do that."

Edward Jones appealed to me for a couple of reasons. First, it was kind of like the military. They had a basic training/boot camp, which was going door to door to build your business. Not everyone could do that. Second, they had a rank structure. They have levels one through ten, and that appealed to me because it gave me a very clear path to become a general in the Edward Jones army. Finally, the major color of Edward Jones at the time was olive drab green, exactly like the army. It was obvious: this must be the right place for me.

There was no top end to how much you can make, so it was a no-brainer. I liked the idea of starting something with no politics, where I could make my own schedule, and where I could help others.

So I reinvented myself again—even though it felt like every part of my life had prepared me for this, from saving money as a little kid to learning new skills to coordinating sports teams, from West Point and the Army to PepsiCo and Phillips 66. I had learned how to associate and get along with people of different backgrounds by going to a diverse military school, then into the Army, and learning how to work with older people onboard the *Queen Elizabeth II*. I learned how to work with franchisees at PepsiCo. It just made all the sense in the world.

So I decided, let's do it.

LEARNING NEW ROPES

I resolved to do everything they told me to do, whatever work was needed to get this business up and running very quickly.

I took the test, did all the pre-study, got accepted, and Karen and I decided to move back to Overland Park, Kansas, a suburb of Kansas City, where it all began after I left the military. We chose Kansas City because it has a low cost of living, people are friendly, and it's easy to get around. All-in-all, Kansas City is a well-kept secret, and to be quite frank, there is a lot to do here.

Karen left her job in Chicago and got another legal secretary job in Kansas City. We bought our first home together, but we decided not to touch any of the money we had left over. Instead, we decided that as we made money with Edward Jones, we would buy furniture one piece at a time. When I first started seeing clients at home, you could hear echoes through the house because the rooms were so bare.

In order to get an office, new Edward Jones recruits had to get to a certain level of production, so I continued to work out of my home. When people came in they'd ask, "Where's your furniture?"

"It's on the way. We just moved from Chicago," I'd say, which was somewhat true. We'd sit and talk at a little fold-out card table, conducting business on folding chairs. I didn't need a fancy office to get people to do business with me.

One day, when it was dead silent, I told Karen, "One of these days, that phone is going to be ringing off the hook."

And within a couple of months, it was.

During that time, I would walk door to door meeting people from eight in the morning until about eight o'clock at night, six or seven days a week. When I got home, Karen would help me input the prospect information into my computer. We worked as a good team to start building the business together.

To tide us over, Karen worked as a legal secretary and I worked part-time in the Kansas National Guard. Once we got the business up and running, that gave us more money to do what we needed to do—and to buy some furniture together.

Over time, I finally got to a level of production where I could move into an office. I finally got an assistant—and then I was off to the races.

We were like two freshly married college kids starting

from scratch, in our first home after moving to a different city and starting a brand-new life. It was very exciting and romantic.

KNOCK, KNOCK

When I first joined Edward Jones, the primary way to meet people and get clients was the door knock. I was taught to go up and down neighborhoods, knocking on doors and introducing myself. Edward Jones trained me how to shake their hand, explain my business, and win them over as clients. The goal was to get as much information as I could about the person who answered the door—the prospect. If I could figure out their concerns, I could help them solve those concerns.

"Hi, my name is Tim Carlin, and I'm opening a new office of Edward Jones in the neighborhood. What's your name?"

"Cecilia."

"Hi, Cecilia. How did I catch you home today?"

"Well, I have three kids and my husband's at work."

"Well, here's a brochure with some information on my company. Is there anything that concerns you right now about college for the kids?"

She might say, "Well, really my husband handles that."

"Would it be possible to give him a call at some point? I'm opening a financial services office, and we help with college planning."

Depending on what she said, I might offer college planning, retirement planning—anything, based on how the conversation went.

In conversations like that, I had to put my ego on the shelf. I was in my mid-forties, a former Fortune 500 executive and division artillery commander in the Kansas Army National Guard, and I faced a lot of rejection going door to door. The people behind the doors didn't know me. They didn't care about what I'd done in the past. They wanted to know why I was knocking on their door. "What do you want?"

Nothing can prepare you for going door to door. It's unnatural. The first time I walked up to knock on a stranger's door, I was dressed in a suit with my shoes perfectly shined. I had my pen and paper. I had been trained on what to do—but you can't really learn everything, because you don't know exactly what's going to happen. You have to think on your feet. My heart was bursting out of my chest, just like when I was back in the military and getting ready to jump out of a plane. That fear is normal. I have the same ordinary fear that everybody has—and I had to do it over and over again.

For every twenty-five doors I knocked on, only maybe one or two people would be home—or willing to open the door and talk to me. My training told me that I had to knock on a thousand doors over the course of a year, just to get a hundred people to talk to me. Of those hundred people, maybe only twenty would eventually become clients. When you first meet people, they're not going to become a client right away. I had to contact them six to twelve more times, every two weeks, until they became a client.

I wanted to improve the odds in my favor, so I went to the Chamber of Commerce and got maps of all the neighborhoods near my office. I marked off the streets indicating the date and time I'd been there. That allowed me to go back to that neighborhood and street on different days and times, so I could eventually meet everyone.

I was getting rejected on so many different fronts—people didn't answer the door, or they slammed it in my face, or they wouldn't give me any information to work with, or they'd say no before I could even tell them how I could help them—but I never gave up. I had the willpower and foresight to see that if I could just work through this and not be afraid of the rejection, if I could keep up the energy to keep going back and knocking on doors until enough people talked to me, I could build this business. Every no meant that I was one step closer to a yes!

Edward Jones required its new advisors to sign on ten new accounts per month. In the first year, I averaged fifty new accounts per month. I tried to knock on two to three thousand doors that first year. This drive really paid off for me. The second year, I opened an average of thirty-eight accounts a month, and the third year, I averaged thirty-five per month. My business grew so fast because I was motivated and it didn't matter to me how small the client's investment was.

At the end of two-and-a-half years, I had approximately 1,200 accounts—more than two-and-a-half times what was expected of me. Most people had 250. My accounts weren't really big, but they were accounts. All together I had about $35 million under management and was made a limited partner, not because of the size of my book of business but because of the potential the company saw in me. I had replaced the income I'd lost when I was laid off—and more than doubled it in a relatively short period of time.

But it was only because I never gave up after all the rejection.

I've talked to other people who wanted to get into this business—full colonels, general officers, or former business executives—but once I told them that you have to start by knocking on doors, they just didn't want to do it. It takes a tremendous amount of mental courage to knock on doors, go back again, see them when they're cutting the grass and go over to say hi, knowing that nobody initially wants to talk to a stranger.

I also had to see the bigger picture, which I've talked about previously too. I couldn't just hear the no or see the closed door right in front of my face—I had to see the *possibility* of a client.

Some of those people whose doors I knocked on are still my clients today. I knocked on David Smith's door, and he or his wife, Katherine, would answer. Whenever they had a question, I would bring them some material. At the time, they had investments with A. G. Edwards. Katherine told me what she said to her husband: "You know, the A. G. Edwards advisor never calls you. This gentleman is contacting you every two weeks, either in person or by phone. You should give him a chance."

David still made me work for it—he asked more questions, and I saw him about twelve times before he finally became a client. We've become good friends, and he's been a great client ever since.

Even now, I call people who decided not to use my services when they were prospects, to remind them that it's a good time to stress test their portfolios. Most of them say, "I am perfectly happy with my financial advisor. We've had a great run for the last ten years."

That's where I say, "That's exactly why now may be the time to conduct a third-party review. There may be some gaps you're not aware of. A stress test doesn't mean you have to leave your advisor, but at least I can give you some ideas that may improve your plan."

No one wants to do a stress test when everything's going well and the Dow is at 28,000—but that's exactly when you *should* do it. But how many people are willing to rock the boat when everything's good? Again, that's why I have to be pleasantly persistent and never give up.

As a US Army Ranger, you plan for what can go wrong and have a contingency to fix it. As a wrestler, when your first move is stopped, you go to your second, third, fourth, or back to your first move until something works. You must be relentless and accept rejection and resistance and do whatever it takes to overcome it.

TIM 2.0

My office at Edward Jones was on the seventh floor of a fourteen-story office building. Back in 2007, a gentleman from the New York Life office on the eighth floor kept coming down to my floor to use the restroom. For whatever reason, whenever we would go in the restroom after he had been in there, we saw that the commode was not being flushed.

After a couple of months of this, the situation got old and we decided we had to do something.

The next time the guy came down to use our restroom *again*, my partner came into my office and let me know. I leaped up from my chair and sprinted down the hallway to the restroom. I pulled out some rough, brown paper towels from the dispenser and wet them in the sink. Then, with all the skill I could muster from my time as an artillery officer, I launched the soggy paper towel bomb over the door and into the stall.

The resonating splat let me know that the projectile had found its target. Although I heard the paper towel land and hit somebody, I didn't hear a word from the gentleman.

I went back to my desk, laughing quietly to myself at the juvenile antics.

About an hour later, I had to go to the restroom myself. I started urinating and noticed a little red tint to my flow. I thought nothing of it and went back to work.

I drink a lot of water, so another hour or so later, I had to go to the restroom again. This time, my urine was a much darker red. I didn't think too much of it because I felt fine. I had also had cranberry juice to drink that day and, although I'd never heard of it happening before, I thought that perhaps the dark red juice was coloring my urine.

That night, I went to a Bikram yoga class and told the teacher, "Hey, if I pass out or anything, call 911 because I may be urinating blood." (As you know, I have a military background—I don't freak out easily.)

I made it through hot yoga and had to urinate afterward. I decided to capture it in my plastic water bottle to check the color, and I saw that it was beet red. It wasn't getting any better, so I went to the Kansas University Medical Center right down the street from my yoga class and said, "I think I'm urinating blood." This was February, so a dozen or so people were there for colds or the flu. They all looked at me funny. Maybe it was the bottle of bright-red liquid I was carrying around.

A nurse took the bottle and, after a few minutes, came back and moved me to the head of the line. They immediately did a cystoscopy, a test to check my bladder. On a man's anatomy, in order to see the bladder, a thin wire with a microscopic camera is inserted into the urethra and up and around the prostate.

I felt totally vulnerable on my back lying in a women's gynecology exam table with my feet up in the stirrups. I felt like I was being abducted by aliens who were taking samples and specimens to do research on the human race. I remember having to wiggle my toes to relax my muscles, to allow the scope to continue its insidious journey.

The doctor finally came back in and told me, "You have a tumor in your bladder."

I said, "Oh, good. It's not cancerous then?" I don't know why I thought that.

"No," the doctor replied, "I think it's a stage-one cancer."

When I heard that, I almost couldn't believe it. I was in shock, devastated, and frightened.

Bladder cancer is the fourth-leading cause of death among men. The tumor typically looks like a cauliflower growing in your bladder. When I had jumped up quickly and ran to the bathroom from my office, the sudden movement had caused a little piece of the cauliflower to flake off, which caused the bleeding. A lot of men may have a little blood in their urine once or twice without ever realizing that it's bladder cancer. Others might have no symptoms at all, and then this cancer keeps growing in your bladder until it invades your wall lining and gets to the kidney and the liver. That's where it gets really difficult to treat.

I was fortunate to get a diagnosis so early; that made treatment much easier and more effective. The next day, I went back to the office, right up to the eighth floor, and found the gentleman from New York Life. "You saved my life," I told him. "And I was the one who dive-bombed you yesterday. I apologize."

He laughed and apologized for using our bathroom so much. I told him that if he hadn't, I wouldn't have found out about the tumor, and that was much more important than flushing.

While I was undergoing treatment for bladder cancer, I surrounded myself with friends and family. I began to eat even better than I already had been and got serious about physical fitness. I took a step back from my business and made sure to get more rest. That gave me more special powers that maybe I didn't have before this bladder cancer, like listening to my body more closely—but it took that triggering event for this to happen.

In a lot of ways, I made lemonade out of lemons. Sometimes, when you're mad at a funny or bad situation, it can actually turn out really good for you. Unfortunately, we all go through crises of some sort. Some of them, like cancer, are out of our control.

After all that, it did turn out to be a stage-one cancer, I completed all my treatment, and today I am cancer free.

CHAPTER 7

Don't Follow
the Crowd

After two-and-a-half years of building my financial service business, I had about 1,200 accounts and $35 million under advisement. That was when I decided to bring in a partner to handle four hundred of those accounts, about $10 million of my business.

When I told my wife, Karen, that I was preparing to give away half my accounts and 33 percent of the dollar amount I had under management, she looked at me like I was crazy. "Are you absolutely out of your mind?" she asked. "You've worked seven days a week, practically twenty-four hours a day to get those accounts, and now you're going to *give them away?*"

I told her, "I think I have a plan. If I transition them, I'll be able to focus on accounts with more sophisticated problems. I'll grow my business back within a year—plus it'll help the new advisor get started, and it's good for the clients because they receive better service."

I went ahead and reduced the accounts I managed from a total of $35 million to $25 million. A year later, I was back up—and more, to $40 million. My theory proved true.

So I did it again two years later. And again. And again and again and again.

PUSHING THE ENVELOPE

This wasn't the first time somebody thought I was crazy for doing something different than everybody else, but I learned long ago that you don't have to do what everybody else does. You don't have to follow the crowd. Instead, you can be a free thinker. You still want to follow the rules, but you also have the opportunity to be independent— and to think independently.

If you get stuck in group-think—going along with what those around you do—it closes your mind to new ideas. Instead, when you do things a little differently, it opens you up to potential for a lot of reward—for yourself and others. When you rely on yourself rather than going along with everyone else, you're much more likely to make the best decision for *you*.

I like to think of myself as very open-minded. I'm always cognizant of what's black and white. I don't violate boundaries intentionally, but I'm an entrepreneur, and I'll push the envelope if I think it can help someone.

When I was younger, I stuck to the letter of the law and was a follower. As I got older, however, in my late teens and early twenties, I realized that sometimes nice guys finish last. That's when I realized that sometimes I can be *too* nice—and that's when I developed some self-confidence, got a little edgier, and started taking risks. Even though I was at West Point, which was a very regimented college, I knew it was time to start pushing the rules a little bit.

My first real girlfriend was another cadet who was a year behind me. We lived in opposite wings of Pershing Barracks, which was a six-story granite building topped with parapets.

After "taps" at eleven, you have to be in your own room. You definitely aren't supposed to be in a room with a member of the opposite sex. But I knew that the fifth floor of the barracks was empty, so we'd often sneak up there after taps.

One night, the officer in charge came into the building to make sure everything was quiet—and that everybody was where they were supposed to be, either in bed or studying. It was so quiet that I could hear his footsteps as he walked through the building making sure everyone was in their room.

We froze. My heart was pounding, and I could feel that hers was too.

Fortunately, he only walked through the third floor and went back downstairs and out the door. He never made it to the fifth floor. We heard the big, wooden door shut, and then we heard him walking on the concrete steps back to his headquarters.

Whew, dodged another bullet!

I wasn't a troublemaker, but having a girlfriend on campus was one of those things that made life at West Point a whole heck of a lot better!

Another time, after I was in the Army, a sergeant came to me and asked to borrow a hundred dollars. That was a lot of money back in 1984 for a second lieutenant, and we weren't supposed to lend money, but he told me what was going on, why he needed the money, and I helped him out.

"Thank you, sir," he told me. "I'll pay you back."

The next day, he went AWOL (which stands for absent without leave).

I never got the money back, but I always felt good because I helped somebody who must have needed it more than I did—and I'm always willing to bend or break the rules if it will help somebody.

The rest of this chapter isn't about pushing the envelope. Instead, I want to share some stories with you about times that I decided to go against the accepted way of doing things—those times I marched (in formation, no less!) to the beat of my own drum.

ADIOS TO THE ARMY

In 1990, my tour of duty was coming to an end and I decided to leave the military. Promotion became too political, and what I felt was minutia became aggravating. The last three years of active duty had been a letdown after the first five. They weren't bad necessarily, but the Army felt too confining and I knew I'd fallen out of love with the military.

My dad tried to dissuade me. "You've got a sure thing with the Army, Tim. You should think twice about walking away from it."

"My heart's just not in it anymore."

And it wasn't—I needed to move on. I retired from active duty at the rank of captain.

I went through a headhunting firm for junior military officers and interviewed to join PepsiCo. However, I missed the comradery and service to the nation, so I joined the Kansas Army National Guard in 1991. Fortunately, I fell back in love with the military then, and I stayed in the National Guard until I retired in 2006 at the rank of full colonel.

HELLO, FINANCIAL SERVICES

That wasn't the last time I would decide not to follow the crowd. Deciding to start my Edward Jones business was a big move in a direction of my own choosing. I went from making a salary—a sure thing—to starting from zero every month with commission- and fee-based sales. That was a big change.

Instead of just doing stocks, bonds, and mutual funds, I chose to also do annuities, disability insurance, life insurance, and long-term care insurance. I also made sure clients were connected with tax and estate-planning professionals, so everyone was talking to one another. If I just wanted to do what everybody else was doing, I would have stuck with investments and taken on more and more accounts. Instead, I wanted to have fewer accounts and do more with them—even if those insurance policies take longer to figure out with a client.

I also got certified in other areas outside of direct financial services, like business owner exit planning. I took a year-long course and exam to get certified in helping business owners sell their businesses when they want, to whom they choose, to live the life they deserve. Not many advisors get certified in that, so it taught me how to integrate all these different people—family therapists, business valuation experts, merger-acquisitions attorneys, investment bankers, estate planning attorneys, accountants, employee stock option plan (ESOP) experts, business analytics experts, Medicare specialists, pension specialists, real estate specialists, reverse mortgage specialists, and Social Security analysts—and coordinate everyone in monthly meetings to help business owners with value building and exit planning.

I'm able to do a total client profile, which is a visual representation of their values, goals, and interests that I can show to a team of experts and get answers to my clients' questions, whether about tax mitigation, wealth transfer, lowering the risk of being sued, and charitable giving. Just as an artillery officer coordinates a mission, or a restaurant manager expedites to serve everyone in a restaurant, or a quarterback directs his team to get the down, I lead my clients to success with their finances, businesses, and life goals because I make sure everyone talks to one another.

Everything I've done has helped me open up a new area of providing value and service to clients and other centers of influence.

MOVING ON UP

As I mentioned in the last chapter, when I first started with Edward Jones, I had to meet my clients in my home. When I reached a certain production level, however, Edward Jones provided me with an office.

At that time, the offices Edward Jones provided for its advisors were most often located in strip malls. I stayed in a small office for two years, but once that lease was up, I wanted something more. I knew I wanted to upscale my business—to make it look and feel higher end, the way I wanted to present myself to clients—so I really needed to be in an upscale office building.

I decided to invest in myself—and in my business. I put in $70,000 of my own money to build out an office in a nice high-rise. It allowed me to elevate my firm's image and propelled my business forward. I was the first person in an Edward Jones office in a high-rise building in Kansas City. I had to have the regional leader come out and approve it. It was different than what everybody else was doing, but he was a forward-thinking guy, and he said, "You know what? Why not? I like the idea."

After that, everyone else followed suit, and Edward Jones stopped putting people in strip malls.

This may seem counterintuitive—especially coming from a financial advisor—but I wasn't risking anybody else's money. Instead of just taking whatever Edward Jones had to offer, I was willing to invest in the style I wanted to have, and that allowed me to put my best foot forward.

GOOD-KNIGHT PLANNING

As I told you earlier, I made the decision to give away $10 million in assets and a lot of accounts in order to grow my business with fewer but deeper relationships. People were surprised that I did that; it was an unconventional move to give away assets after only two-and-a-half years in the business. But by asset sharing, I knew that I would grow the business and that more families would be serviced by the quality advisors I selected to be my partners. And by giving away even *more*, I grew even bigger.

Every time I transitioned business—and over time I've

done about seven giveaways, or good-knight plans—more came back to me. I was able to bring in quality partners to reduce the number of households I worked with directly. Again, this may seem counterintuitive, but giving away business allowed me to focus on clients with increasingly sophisticated needs and ultimately to get more business. I didn't make the decision out of fear or greed. This transition was also good for my clients. Instead of being forgotten among hundreds of accounts, they continued to receive monthly proactive contact from my partners.

I know that I'm serving the right people, and ultimately I have more time to give back to them—and to Karen and myself. Work isn't stressful; it's fulfilling.

Now, I'm working with the clients I enjoy most and who enjoy working with me. My clients are generally independent people like me, kind, caring people who want to save money to have more time and freedom to do what they want. I am fortunate enough to have surrounded myself with people who love their families and want to use their money to make sure those families are safe and protected.

My ideal clients like to have a personal relationship; we become friends and do things together outside of the business. We'll have a glass of wine and talk about what's going on in the world—or their children, families, or hopes and dreams of what they're going to do when they retire. Maybe they want to get together to watch football or baseball, or—as with the clients I told you about in the introduction—they'll invite my wife and me to family gatherings for Halloween, Thanksgiving, Christmas, or a wedding celebration.

These are the kind of clients I've built my business on— and, in turn, they trust that I'll help them reach their goals.

A good financial advisor helps people. If you grow a client's $100,000 to $1 million, help them retire, protect their principle, and get them set up with a family foundation for their kids—then you're worth your weight in gold.

Growing wealth is an ability; it takes training, education, and hard work. Some people think that if they just give a little time and attention, they can do anything: pitch in the major leagues, be an American Idol, become an Army Ranger. But accomplishment at high levels requires abilities that experts train and practice years to attain. The same is true for managing finances.

My clients like that I'm always thinking of new ideas to help solve their problems. They want advice, someone to guide them and tell them why they should consider making certain decisions. The things they like about me are the things that set me apart from other financial planners, the things that keep me hungry for more.

WHY NOT ME?

Before I gave away clients to my partners, I asked myself, "Why should I sit back and be happy with where I am when I can have the opportunity to create more jobs by bringing in more assets and people, then connecting them with people who can help them even more?"

Somebody has to serve the high-net-worth clients. Why not me?

So I did.

I have reinvented myself, growing and changing rather than staying stuck in one place. There are very few politics involved. I can have the clients I like, really develop friendships with people I care about, and spend time serving them. People depend on me—and they know I'll be there for them, whether they're getting ready to retire, or if they get a divorce, or when someone passes away. It's really nice to spend time with them and put their fears at ease so they feel comfortable going through a life transition like that.

It's no different than when I was dancing, looking in the eyes of the older women who had been through so much in life, and giving them a magical moment. These days, I'm looking at folks who are moving from being very intensely involved in their jobs to stepping off a ledge and going into retirement, making sure they know they're safe and protected for the rest of their lives. If you can look in their eyes and give them that same feeling, they know they're going to be okay.

WHAT'S YOUR HAPPY PLACE?

Ultimately, I wanted to work in the environment I *wanted* to be in.

What makes you happy? What's your happy place?

If the military had been my happy place, I would have stayed in the military full-time. But I had a curiosity to learn about growing my own business. I wasn't afraid to work to do both, and I did as long as that made sense.

I wasn't afraid to build out my office. Now I'm on the sixth floor, I have a corner office, and I look out over this beautiful area. I can come and go when I want. I created my own happy place and my own reality where my clients can be happy too.

Because I've built my business to support how I want my life to be, when I meet with my clients, I can spend as much time as I need to. I don't have hundreds of clients; I have a select group of clients that I can focus on, allowing me to serve them better and enjoy our time together more.

There are no guarantees in life, but anything that can give you a little bit more time to do what you want to do, to be in your happy place, is a good thing.

Then, once you've found your happy place, the most important thing you can do is give back to others and help them find their happy places as well.

CHAPTER 8

You Have to Give to Receive

People often ask if my wife and I have children. Usually, I say, "We couldn't conceive," and leave it at that. That's the truth, but I want to tell you the story of how we found out.

In a perfect world, you meet someone, fall passionately in love, get married, and have kids. That's the way it's meant to be—but that's not the way it worked for me and Karen.

When we got married, neither of us had children, and we wanted to start a family together. We tried to get pregnant the natural way, but after a couple of years of trying with no results, we decided that we should test our fertility. I called and made an appointment at Shawnee Mission Medical Center.

"Should I plan to go with you?" Karen asked me.

"No, I'll be fine," I told her.

I would have to provide a semen sample, but that wouldn't be a problem. I imagined that they'd show me into a nice, comfortable room with dim lighting, pop in a DVD, and hand me a couple of magazines. Nothing to it.

When I arrived for the appointment, I was dressed to the hilt in a suit and tie, my camelhair coat slung casually over one arm. After a few minutes in the waiting room, a nurse escorted me down a hallway and opened the door to the room where I'd have to procure my sample.

Instead of the warm, inviting room I'd envisioned, she showed me into one of the gynecological exam rooms. There was a table with stirrups, bright florescent lighting overhead, and a cold tile floor. The nurse handed me an eight-ounce cup, gave me a stack of papers to fill out, and showed me the intercom button. "When you're ready, call me," she said as she walked out the door.

"You've got to be kidding me," I thought. Superman couldn't even fill that cup—let alone a forty-five-year-old man in a sterile exam room. There wasn't a TV in sight, much less a stack of DVDs. I felt relieved when I saw a pile of magazines, but that feeling quickly disappeared as I flipped through them: *Good Housekeeping, Time, Newsweek.* What was I supposed to do with any of those? Where were the girly magazines??

I started to panic.

I threw magazines aside, digging through the stack. I found an old issue of *People* magazine, but that wasn't going to do it either. I pulled open drawers and rummaged through the cabinets like a drug addict looking for an errant pill.

Finally, I picked up the stack of paperwork and found a stash of dirty magazines at the bottom. *Okay, now we're getting somewhere.*

Fifteen minutes later, I was done with what I had to do. My sample was at the bottom of the huge cup. I couldn't resist teasing the nurse.

"Miss," I called over the intercom, "can you please come down here? Make it fast—the cup is overflowing!"

"Oh my god," she exclaimed. "I'll be right there!"

I heard the pounding of feet as she rushed madly down the hall. When she opened the door, I was fully dressed and smiling.

"Just teasing," I said. "The cup is on top of the papers."

My test results came back, and I was above average in everything: I had a high count of healthy sperm. They were swimming so well, they practically jumped off the petri dish.

After much anguish and the consideration of adoption, Karen and I left it at that. We'd been trying to get pregnant for so long and, at that point, she just didn't want to go any further. We didn't want to go through the emotional stress of the in vitro process.

We'd both helped raise our siblings when we were younger because we were the oldest kids in our families and our parents needed our support. Neither of us had the typical, carefree childhood. Ours were full of responsibility, and we had to be adults from such a young age that, quite frankly, we were a little burned out. If it had happened naturally, we would have had children, but now we have the ability to never stand still. It's never boring because we're involved in so many other things and living life to the fullest.

Most people are understanding when they hear that we couldn't have kids. I've never gotten askance looks over that. We're just humans, after all; we're not perfect people—we're ordinary. Not getting everything you want is part of life.

At times, all of us have probably been guilty of looking at other people's lives and feeling jealous or envious because we think their lives are perfect. Nobody's life is perfect. We all have challenges—they're just different for everybody.

I'm a long way from my days as a paperboy in Buffalo, but the path from there to here is connected. From Canisius to West Point, from the traditions set by my mom and dad to the values instilled in me by the US Army—it has all made me the person I am today. I established good habits. I worked hard and saved money from each paycheck, and that continues to this day.

Could I go out and buy that dream house now? Sure. But I won't, not until I can afford it without dipping into my savings.

Being financially successful allows me to determine my own destiny. Money allows you to make decisions based on what will bring you happiness and a sense of fulfillment. Having money in and of itself is not so important; it's the freedom of choice it allows.

And to me, the most important option money provides is the opportunity to give back to others.

GIVING BACK TO MY COMMUNITY

Although we don't have children, we're passionate about supporting foster care charities, such as Casa House, which provides foster homes for kids who don't have parents, and Sunflower House, which provides help for abused children who are in a bad situation.

We support the Heart of America Council to help further their cause for young people, and we donate to City Union Mission to help homeless people who need meals, a place to stay, a chance to get a haircut, and to be trained for a job.

I'm a Rotary Club member, and I support the Parkinson's Foundation and the Live for Joy Foundation, which is for myeloma, a type of eye cancer.

We believe in Wayside Waifs and the KC Pet Project, which is a no-kill shelter to help animals who have been abused or abandoned, giving them a chance to be protected and maybe adopted into their forever home.

SUNDAY SURPRISES

When I was growing up, my dad would often plan a special outing for the whole family. He called these outings "Sunday surprises," but they could happen any day of the week. Usually, we went to dinner at a family-owned Greek or Italian restaurant. That's where we learned to keep our elbows off the table, use the proper fork, and mind our manners. We were taught how to behave in different settings.

For some outings, we dressed up to the nines and went to the theater, the ballet, or the symphony. That instilled a lifelong appreciation in me for culture and the arts.

Other times, we explored a new beach, like Evangola State Park, or took a day trip to Fort Niagara to see a reenactment of the American Indian Wars. Once we even drove to Toronto and spent two nights in a hotel.

I loved Sunday surprises because they meant that we were all together as a family, which could be tough to manage because of my dad's odd hours as a police officer. On those days, though, we all crammed into the family car, and I knew that we could be going just about anywhere.

To this day, I like to get dressed up and attend the ballet and the theater—even if it's no longer a surprise!

Karen and I share a love of the arts, and we support arts organizations, such as the Broadway Education Alliance and the Kansas City Ballet, because we believe that the arts provide enrichment and well-roundedness beyond basic education.

TO SERVE AND SUPPORT

The high school I attended in Buffalo was focused on providing education in the Catholic tradition of community service. Canisius continues to do a lot of mission work helping the less fortunate by providing strong academic, religious, and social experiences. I believe it's important to support faith-based organizations for all the good they do in the community helping the homeless and disenfranchised.

I had a wonderful experience during my time at Canisius, and I want to help them continue to serve others. I give to the school itself and also contribute to the wrestling team because it played such an important role in making me who I am today. Wrestling isn't as flashy a sport as football, but it taught me tremendous discipline, self-control, and confidence.

I also contribute to West Point because it taught me the kind of values that have made me a better person to serve others as a military officer. West Point showed me the importance of duty, honor, and country. We have a duty to service. A cadet is honorable. A cadet will not lie, cheat, steal, nor tolerate those who do. I believe in our country. I love democracy and discourse, even if it's a bit like making sausage: the process may not look good, but the end result is worth it.

I'm sharing this not to pat myself on the back or to look like a good guy. These are my core beliefs. Giving back in service to others has been a way of life for me since I was an altar boy at Assumption Church.

I support causes that are important to my clients and family. People tend to support organizations that feel personal to them, such as medical research into illnesses that may have touched a family member. It's a way of not forgetting about a loved one who has passed away. We owe it to these people to keep their memories alive, to help fund a cure or find ways to control a disease. So whenever I see a friend, family member, or client going through a medical issue, I always find a way to contribute however I can. If a client has lost a loved one unexpectedly, or to cancer or Parkinson's or another illness, giving in their name feels like the right thing to do.

The worst thing we can do for someone who has passed away is forget them. The best thing we can do for someone we've lost is to honor them by supporting the causes that helped them or that they believed in.

Conclusion

Shortly before I turned forty, I thought, "Hey, I'm not getting any younger. I've always wanted to run a marathon—and I'd better seize the moment before it gets too late in life!"

I don't want to leave anything on the table.

I wasn't really a runner—I run a couple of miles every other day to keep fit, but nothing like the long-distance race I was going to attempt. I'm not built like a runner; I'm built more like a wrestler—short and muscular. So I'm not the fastest or most efficient runner, but I knew that if I broke up the process into small pieces I could grind it out.

Once I decided to run, I chose the Walt Disney World Marathon. I followed a twenty-six-week training plan to be ready in time—and, as I'm sure you know about me by now, I followed it to the letter. The first day, I ran two miles. The next day, I ran two and a half. The third day, I ran three miles, but on the fourth day, I went back down to two miles. After that, I took a day off and then did a five-mile run on day six. It's a stair-step progressive training program.

I'm not like Forrest Gump, who is (a) fictional and (b) can pick up and run forever. I need to have the system to follow and, with my discipline, good things will happen.

Even with a plan in place, training was still hard. After a while, I realized, "Wow, I'm going to run twenty-six miles." In training, the longest run I had to do was twenty miles. On race day, I was going to have to do that—and then I'd *still* have six miles to go.

There were days when I wanted to quit. I didn't *have* to run a marathon, so why was I dragging myself out of bed at five-thirty in the morning in cold weather? I thought back to my days as an altar boy, forcing myself to get up early and crunch a mile through the snow to that altar. I may not have wanted to do it—but I did it. And I knew I could do it again.

I did it because there's a rainbow at the end. I did it because it was the right thing to do. I did it because I set a goal, made a commitment, and I was going to follow through on it. I do what I say I'm going to do, and I'm loyal to my goals—just like I'm loyal to the people I want to keep as friends. It was still a grind, but I tried to keep my positive attitude. I knew that even though it may not always be smooth, and there would be literal and figurative bumps in the road, I'd get through it and feel better about myself for having done so.

Just like writing this book, building my business, finishing Ranger School, or learning to dance, I didn't always look forward to every part of it, but in the end I love the results.

The day of the marathon, I woke up at four-thirty in the morning in Orlando, Florida. I was full of energy for the 26.2 miles ahead of me; I was just so excited—and half that excitement was because I was going to get to run through Disney World, Epcot Center, and the theme parks in that area. It was going to be so cool to do that on my first marathon run. I had been to the theme parks before, but now I was going to run through them with no one in the park but us runners—and some spectators and Disney characters like Mickey, Minnie, and Goofy, who came out to give us high fives.

We were put in different holding pens depending on our time—people who run a five-minute mile were together, and people who run a ten-minute mile were together in another group. You start the race with your group so you're not holding up people who are faster than you. We started running at six, still in the dark. It was cool when we started—it was central Florida in January at six in the morning, so it was about thirty-nine degrees—but then it warmed up.

I felt so good through the race. It was fun, and I'd done the training. I felt confident that the training had worked; I believed in the system, which—along with being positive—is important to making it through a marathon. I knew that if I followed my training, I would finish that marathon—and I did, coming in a little under four hours. My parents and sister came down from New York, and they were there cheering for me at the finish line. So fun!

I was so proud of finishing that marathon. A couple of years later, I ran the Chicago Marathon too. The first one was the best, though, because it was so exciting.

Walt Disney World 1999 marathon.

ALL PART OF THE PROCESS

Being ordinary, physical stuff comes easier to me than
activities that take a lot of thought or time for intro-

spection. But what helped take me to the level of an extraordinary achievement is that I'm not afraid to put myself out there and try a marathon, even though I'm not a runner. Even though I'm not an author, I'm trying to write a book.

Not everyone is willing to put themselves out there, to put in the time, effort, and energy necessary to actually go through the process and see it all the way through. Not everyone is willing to share their story, or they think they don't have a story—but we all do. We just have to be willing to follow the process.

Now that you've read many of the experiences I've had in different facets of my life—whether as an altar boy, dancing, being in the military, building a financial advisory practice, or delivering newspapers as a boy in Buffalo during a blizzard—you know that nothing is going to intimidate me. I've seen it all and made it through my personal challenges, whether they've been fun, like running a marathon, or not as much fun, like surviving bladder cancer.

Life isn't all fun. It's full of ordinary events—getting sick, getting divorced, making bad decisions, losing a job—but those events can also become extraordinary opportunities to learn, grow, and achieve great success without having it handed to us.

Some people say, "Oh, I don't know if I want to go through that process."

There are people who don't want to pay the price for their success, whether that price is physical, emotional, mental, or time. But when we pay the price to get through a challenge, even though it isn't easy, we find an opportunity—an opportunity to be extraordinary.

People don't always want to fight through the pain. They're looking for a silver bullet, but it doesn't exist. Everything is a marathon. When you've been exposed to the world, you understand what it takes to follow a process, see it through, and run a marathon to reach your goal.

If you live in Buffalo, New York, all your life and never get out and see what's happening in the rest of the world—even if you're the mayor of Buffalo—that's ordinary. But if you go out and do all these different things, you may still be ordinary, but you will have had some extraordinary experiences that even the mayor may not have had.

You can be an ordinary person with problems, fears, doubts, failings, and flaws, but still find a solution to fix them, without fixating on the past. You can make that delicious, sugar-free lemonade out of all the lemons life tosses your way.

If you're willing to work through the pain, to follow the

whole process and see it through, it's possible for all of us to reinvent ourselves into something extraordinary.

So how do we do it? By keeping an open mind, understanding that there's not just one right way of doing things, understanding that life is a series of peaks and valleys. It takes being empathetic to others, apologizing when you're wrong, and trying to put your ego on the shelf.

But the number-one key to accomplishing something extraordinary is having discipline.

DISCIPLINE IS FREEDOM

One of the things that many people lack today is a certain degree of discipline.

I'm not overly disciplined—I have fun, eat ice cream, and stay out late dancing sometimes. But 80 percent of the time, I'm pretty disciplined. And having that discipline gives me freedom.

When I was an altar boy, it took discipline to get up and go to church before six in the morning. Watching my food intake to make weight as a wrestler took discipline. I was depriving myself a little bit for a greater good. When I went to West Point and had to sit one fist away from my chair, square corners when I walked, and could only speak freely in the privacy of my room—all of that required some degree of discipline.

Not everyone necessarily has, or needs, that level of discipline. But having the determination and dedication to do all that—in addition to dollar cost averaging every month, coming to work even when I didn't want to, and knocking on doors even after facing rejection again and again—ultimately gave me the greatest gift of all: the freedom at this point in my life to do what I want.

Discipline frees you from bad habits and guilt.

You don't have to follow the crowd, you don't have to do what everybody else does, you don't have to be the number-one person on social media—you can do things that are good for you, but you have to have some mental discipline to do so. At first it may seem very restrictive, but over time it's very freeing and opens up a world of different opportunities. Discipline provides security— physically, mentally, spiritually, and financially—to do whatever you may want to achieve.

When you make discipline part of your long-term thinking, it becomes easier to plan your future and reach the freedom you ultimately want. You know what you're doing and why you're doing it. Discipline serves as motivation to make it through to your ultimate goal.

A WORD ON THE COVID-19 CRISIS

I'd be remiss if I didn't mention the COVID-19 pandemic occurring during this dramatic time in our country's history.

Although our country goes through a significant event every eighty to one hundred years that changes the course of our history, many of us have never experienced a pandemic like the one previous generations faced in 1918.

Even without prior experience to fall back on, we are all becoming extraordinarily ordinary during this time.

Like I previously mentioned in this book, we are all being in service to others. We continue to learn as the crisis evolves, and we each adapt our own ways of helping one another.

So many of us, especially our heroes on the front lines, are punching above our weight.

America is not standing still. We're trying to improve and learn new things about this virus. We're cognizant of the dangers but fearless and confident in confronting our new reality.

We must continue to think long-term and consider what's important to our future generations.

All of us are reinventing ourselves so we stay relevant to our current environment and the changing situation.

We are in America. We don't need to follow whatever crowd may be out there. We have liberties in our country to make our own decisions. The important thing is to see the full, 360-degree picture and keep an open mind about all of the information that we are given.

And always remember: you have to give to receive.

As we go through this crisis, if we keep these principles in mind, we'll emerge on the other side better, as we did in all of our previous crises: the landing at Plymouth Rock, the Revolutionary War, the Civil War, World War I, the Great Depression, World War II—and now the COVID-19 crisis.

May God bless you and our great country of the United States of America.

YOU ARE EXTRAORDINARY

We all have the potential inside of us to be extraordinary and to do extraordinary things. If we all realized that and trusted in it, the world would be a better place. People wouldn't be so upset, negative, or disappointed by their situations in life. We would all know that we have potential, and we'd put in the time, energy, and effort to achieve the extraordinary.

Never give up. Too many people throw in the towel and accept the fate they've been given. More people die climbing down a mountain than going up. Ascending a mountain is relatively easy because you're using your hips, your gluteus maximus, your calves and thighs. When descending a mountain, however, you only have your front quadriceps; it's much more difficult. When I climbed up Mount Kilimanjaro, I wasn't sore at all. After I came back down, though, I was sore and fatigued for days.

It's easy to get one goal accomplished, but how about the second, third, fourth, and fifth? How do you get more out of life? By using the lessons I've shown you: reinventing yourself, making lemonade out of lemons, and always learning.

Everything happens in life for a reason. It all comes together at a particular time to point you in a certain direction and keep you moving forward. During the writing of this book, my mom passed away. I got in a serious car accident requiring hospitalization. I got a medical diagnosis and had to have my hip replaced, then I transitioned to becoming an independent financial advisor. It may sound like one problem after the other, but none of that derailed me from my life. We take our punches and move on with our plan. I'm never going to be distracted; I want to stay focused on my goal of helping people, regardless of what's happening in my life.

Similarly, if something happens with your plan for getting up the mountain, you can trust that I'll be there to help you get through it, no problem.

Even through the tough times we can still be happy and successful. Don't be afraid of falling in love. Don't let the fear of not finishing a marathon keep you from even starting. Don't be afraid of knocking on doors just because you may be rejected. Don't dwell on the past or negative things that have happened in your life.

Accentuate the opportunities and positive things that have been given to you and drive them to a successful conclusion. There's most likely no one event that will make or break you. You will experience a series of events that, over time, can turn an ordinary life into an extraordinary one.

Are you ready?

Get out there, make a splash, and enjoy your extraordinary life!

Acknowledgments

Thank you to my wife, Karen, for her love and support.

I'm grateful to my mom and dad for giving me a great compass to navigate life and all of its opportunities and challenges.

Thank you to Dr. Steve and Sharon Gerson; my brother, Jeff (aka Cannonball); and my good friend and client, Bob Welborn, for being the first readers of my book and giving me ideas to make it even better.

I also want to thank all my teachers, especially Bill Grotke and Vinnie Chiumento, who have been instrumental in my life, made learning fun, and showed me the importance of being a lifelong learner. They were there when I needed them the most and have had an enormous impact on my life.

Finally, I want to express my gratitude to my clients: without your support, loyalty, and trust in good and bad times, this book would not have been possible. In no particular order, my thanks go to: Gary Rettman, Jerry and Lucy Usry, Tracy, Jim and Connie Leonardelli, Brenda Jacobson, Bruce and Diane Boeger, Hannah Ball, Bob and Jeanene Welborn, Rob Welborn, Christy Welborn, Emery and Jane Rogers, John and Jane Vandewalle, Dr. Steve and Sharon Gerson, Stefani Gerson, Chad and Gouri Chaudhuri, Steve and Julie Bamberger, Tom and Madeline Johnson, Brian Henry and Mary Collins, Mike and Cindy Usry, Jeff and Cheryl Kerns, Matt Kerns, Steve Kerns, Michele Kerns, Wade and Dee Anne Osborne, Danny Chong and Adam Splitter, Tony and Beth Kemper, Rick and Karen Rodenbeck, Dan and Janis Carier, Ted and Valorie Strickler, Roger and Terri Moore, Ryan and Holly Burch, Hank and Mary Gale Kramer, Terri Reynolds, Craig and Danielle Settles, Vinson and Lorie Loos, Gary and Donna Fowler, BG (Ret.) USA Bryan and Jennifer Wampler, Patrick and Justine Termino, Dr. Deb and Tripti Bhaduri, Rick and Diana Poccia, Jerry and Carol Shreve, Bob and Jan Borgelt, Steve and Kay Koffel, LTC (Ret.) USA Patrick and SFC (Ret.) USA Sheila Ryan, LTC (Ret.) USA Jim and CPT (Ret.) USA Deb Hevel, Babe and Laura Kwasniak, Bob and Peg Marland, Paul Egger, Merna Upp, Rob Harken and Stacy Gerson, Jim Mason and Bruce Crane, Bill and Maria Koch, CSM (Ret.) USA Dale and Judy Putman, Aubrey Shreve, Greg and Julie

Jegen, Susie Wolfert, Gary Roles, LTC (Ret.) USA Ron and Peg Nicholl, Joe and Pam Wranich, LTC (Ret.) USA Craig Fox and LTC (Ret.) USA Cheryl Whelan, Barry and Jennifer Scott, Cinthy Wilcox, Barb Drury, COL (Ret.) USA Bill and Carol Vonderschmidt, Rick and Deb Morris, Sunny and Jana Kumar, Terry and Dawn Hoffhines, Larry Ge and Eileen Zhu, Jay and Julia Dunfield, Carol Whelan, Terry and Deb Porter, LTC (Ret.) USA Brian Detoy and Sheryl Shafer, Ram and Saritha Guduputi, LTC (Ret.) USAF Tom and Beate Pettigrew, Sarah Rotman, Rick and Karen Yord, Bill and Becca Yord, Alba Perez, Hugo and Maggie Perez, COL KSARNG John and Carrie Rueger, Kent and Ginger Ewonus, Jordan Ewonus, Kurt and Becky Becker, Jerry Erdmann and Jolene Horsman, CSM (Ret.) USA George and Karyl Stevens, Yagesh and Shashi Kumar, Dave and Joanna Meats, Brian and Linda Rasmussen, Ingrid Sargis, Gary and Jill Usry, Joe and Barb Lewis, Deb Maney, Tom and Kathryn Kahrs, John and Jen Clark, Jim and Lea Winter, Jon and Julie Christiansen, Mark Christiansen, Kevin and Lynn Kruse, Rodney and Diane Haist, Caroline Chong, Joe and Rhonda Kitchner, Mike and Judy Walberg Sr., Mike and Monica Walberg Jr., Diana Farrow-White, Amiee Ford, Heidi McIntyre, and John Carlin.

About the Author

TIM CARLIN is an independent certified financial planner with V Wealth Advisors LLC whose life up to this point has contributed to his definition of success.

Tim graduated from West Point in 1982 and is a twenty-two-year veteran of the US Army and Kansas Army National Guard. He served in the 101st Airborne Division, the 2nd Armored Cavalry Regiment, and the 35th Infantry Division at Battery, Battalion, and Brigade level command.

Upon leaving active duty in 1990, Tim joined the Pepsi-Cola Company and served in various operational and financial roles leading him to become director of franchise operations for KFC Restaurants in Kansas, Oklahoma, and northern Texas. In 1997, he was recruited to take over as the director of national quick service operations for the Phillips 66 Petroleum Company headquartered in Bartlesville, Oklahoma. After helping build out the "Kicks 66" brand, Tim returned to Kansas City and, in 2003, he joined the financial advisory firm of Edward Jones. In 2019, he joined the independent advisory firm of V Wealth Advisors where he currently manages assets for a select group of high-net-worth individuals and business owners throughout the United States.

Tim resides in Overland Park, Kansas, with his wife, Karen, and two four-legged kids, Romeo and Juliet.

Lightning Source UK Ltd.
Milton Keynes UK
UKHW011901100920
369713UK00002B/47/J